The Story of Music

The Story of Music

Text by Nicholas Ingman

Illustrations by Bernard Brett

Ward Lock Limited/London

ISBN 0 7063 1306 2

First published in Great Britain 1972
by Ward Lock Limited, 116 Baker Street,
London, W1M 2BB

Text filmset in 12pt Apollo
by Yendall and Company Limited, London

Printed and bound by
Casterman S.A., Belgium

Sure there is music
even in the beauty, and the
silent note which Cupid
strikes, far sweeter than
the sound of an instrument.
For there is music where
ever there is a harmony,
order, or proportion: and
thus far we may maintain
the music of the spheres.
Sir Thomas Browne
Religio Medici

Contents

Introduction   8

1   Man's Early Voice   10

2   25,000 Years Ago   12

3   The First Musical
    Instruments   14

4   The Music of Ancient
    Persia   16

5   Music of the Bible   18

6   Theory and Practice   20

7   Eastern Music   23

8   Praise Him With Music 26

9   Minstrels and
    Troubadours   30

10 The First Writing of
    Music   33

11 The Oldest Written
    Music   36

12 To the Glory of God   38

13 Organs – Great and
    Small   42

14 Three Early Masters   44

15 The First Operas   46

16 Music – the Food
    of Love   49

17 Bach – the Greatest
    of Them All   50

18 Handel – a Man
    of Society   53

19 Mozart – the
    Four-year-old Genius   55

20 Beethoven – the Deaf
    Composer   59

21 The Early Romantics   64

22 Paganini – the Devil's
    Disciple   68

23 Stradivarius – The
    Violin Maker   69

24 Wagner – Composer
    to the Gods   71

25 The Romantic Opera   73

26 Tchaikovsky – Master
    of the Ballet   76

27 The Last Romantics   78

28 Ballads, Songs
    and Snatches   82

29 The Rebels   84

30 Stravinsky – the
    Frontiersman   86

31 The Twentieth
    Century   88

32 Music in Britain   94

33 The New World   98

34 The Jazz Scene   102

35 Pop – Music of Youth   105

36 Electronic Sounds   110

37 Into the Future   112

38 The Language of
    Music   114

39 Reading a Score   117

40 Instruments of
    the Orchestra   119

Introduction

Whether you are concerned with music as a hobby, or as a subject for serious study, or as just one of those fascinating things around us, it is sincerely hoped you will find something of interest in these pages.

This is not supposed to be a very profound book. It contains no great new thoughts or penetrating analyses of master works. You will not find learned professorial discourses on 'the compound binary form of the sonata', nor even discussions on the 'pandiatonic clusters' of the Beatles' songs. Nor, except for the one short chapter on 'How To Read a Score', is there a single note of written music.

There is a place for all these things, of course, but not in a book written expressly for young people who 'just want to know what it is all about.'

The Story of Music is offered as just that – a story. A story full of fascinating characters, some bizarre, some tragic, some comic – but all of them concerned unswervingly with the one compass point of music.

Here are told the adventures, trials and successes – and some catastrophic failures – of men of tremendous talent, of a flame burning inside them that drove them to sublime heights, sometimes only to fall again disastrously.

The word 'genius' is all too often used carelessly. A true genius is a very rare creature – few of us meet one in our entire lives. And yet this book is stuffed with them – men whose abilities were so far ahead of those of anyone else as to justify the use of the word. Think, for instance, of the child Mozart, playing the harpsichord like a master and composing orchestral works before he was nine. Think of the deaf Beethoven, writing great symphonies which have never been equalled and yet unable to hear a single note of them!

And the eccentricities of some of these men of music! Bruckner, the great composer of Vienna, who habitually walked about in wide floppy trousers cut short at the legs so that he had more freedom for the pedals of his organ, wearing a clown's collar several sizes too big, and shod in odd sized boots, rushing up to the famous and dignified conductor of one of his works and thrusting a shilling into his hand and begging him to buy himself a glass of beer.

The young Robert Schumann, who wanted so badly to be a great pianist that he invented a gadget which he clamped on his wrist to help the movement of his fingers, only to find that it ruined his playing for life.

The tremendously wealthy Mendelssohn family who hired a symphony orchestra every Sunday morning so that their twelve-year-old son could practise his conducting.

Or, again, the virtuoso violinist, Paganini, who was said to be so brilliant that he couldn't possibly be just human, and that he was helped by the Devil, whom a writer of the time swore that he saw standing just behind Paganini during a concert helping the violinist's flying fingers in their unbelievable speed and skill.

There are a hundred tales like these, as well as tales of triumph over immense obstacles, happy stories and sad stories, stories of wealth and stories of poverty – all of them threaded on the single strand of talent.

It is also, although this it did not set out to be, a narrative of changing social conditions, from the time when musicians were mere beggars, not allowed into a decent household, to the time when they were not only accepted but made wealthy and given titles of nobility. From the Biblical times when music was inseparable from worship, through the period when the church banned it completely as being a vulgar and disturbing influence, to the long, long period when the church was the major supporter of music and musicians.

And if you should think that the admiration and tremendous rewards given to modern pop stars are something new, remember that the kithara players of ancient Greece were equally well rewarded in their day, and that the minstrels of the Middle Ages were the companions of kings and princes.

Music has always been an essential part of

man's existence, at all times and in all countries and with all classes.

The object of this book is to tell these exciting events as a *story*. It is not a textbook for learning music – only for learning *about* music.

And remember, there is only one thing better than reading about music – and that is, *listening* to it. It is hoped that after you have read this book you will find that the music itself will be even more interesting and exciting.

Wandering Minstrels *by Dietrich playing the bag pipes and a fiddle c.1700*

*A very early instrument
was the bull roarer*

10

1 Man's Early Voice

Nobody knows how or when music began. However, if we let our imagination reach backwards we can make some reasonable guesses.

From bits of skeletons and man-made objects buried in the earth's crust we can get a fairly clear pattern of how man himself developed. There is no real starting point – just a very gradual, very very slow change over vast periods of time.

We do know from the shape and size of fragments of skull that have been dug up that it was many millions of years before man developed the power of speech. Man's ape-like predecessors could have communicated only by a limited range of grunts and cries, indicating basic emotions like fear, hunger, anger and satisfaction.

It was only about a million years ago that the first true man evolved. He is classed as a 'true' man for many reasons. He walked upright, he had a relatively large brain, he knew the use of fire, he made tools and, most important for us, he developed the power of speech.

Probably his speech had very few words, but they must at least have had ups and downs, loudnesses and softnesses, shorts and longs, and he must have used these variations to express himself.

Imagine him, therefore, at a moment when he has done something that makes him very excited and happy. He has killed an animal for food, or defeated an enemy who attacked him, or had a new baby born to him. Imagine him dancing about, uttering cries of pleasure mixed up with his few words, using his voice in a different way from ordinary speaking. Could we say he was singing?

If we can stretch a point and say that it was singing of a sort; then we have got as near as we are ever likely to get to finding the beginnings of music.

Music probably began with early man uttering cries and stamping his feet to produce rhythms

2 25,000 Years Ago

We must now make a huge jump forward in time – almost a million years on from the last chapter. At first sight the man we are going to meet will not look very different from the last. Yet, in fact, the difference is enormous.

We have now reached Modern Man – but the word 'modern' used in this sense is merely a technical description. He is still a savage, squatting in a cave, hunting animals and unable yet to grow his own food.

But he can speak – and presumably sing – and he is beginning to wonder about all sorts of things. He wonders, for instance, about life after death – he buries his dead with spears and food, thinking perhaps that the departed might need them after he had left this earth.

He wears clothes consisting of skins roughly stitched together with bone needles. His skin is light coloured and his features are not very different from the European of today. Sometimes he lived in caves, but as often as not he built tents of a rough sort or dug holes in the ground and roofed them over with skins covered with earth. He had not yet got round to farming although he had learned to gather in food that grew wild, as well as hunt animals.

The most interesting thing about early man is that he was a very accomplished artist. Almost from the beginning man has made attempts at carving stones or scratching patterns on them, but this fellow – we call him 'Cro-Magnon Man' because that is the name of the village in Southern France where remains of this kind of man were first found – had gone far beyond such primitive attempts at art.

He had learned to paint, using colours made from earths and clays mixed with animal fat, and applied them with sticks and even primitive brushes. Occasionally he used dry colours by blowing them on to the rock face through a hollow bone. The colouring was absorbed into the limestone, which accounts for the fact that

Oldest-known drawing of a musical instrument

his paintings are still brilliant and vivid 25,000 years after they were painted. These paintings are found in many caves in Southern France and Northern Spain and are seen by thousands of tourists every year.

What is important about these paintings in the story of music is that one of them shows the first ever drawing of a musical instrument. In the cave of 'The Three Brothers', at Arriège, near the Pyrenees Mountains in Southern France, there is a wall drawing that has become famous as 'The Magus' (The Magician). It shows a figure which is part man, part animal – perhaps meant to represent a primitive medicine man, or magician, dressed in animal skins. What is specially important about it is that the figure is holding a bow, one end in its mouth, with the right hand in a plucking position. The implication of this is that primitive man had found out that if one end of the bow was held in the teeth the mouth acted as a sound box and amplified the sound. Also, that by altering the tension on the bow the sound could be changed up or down. Quite a discovery 25,000 years ago!

Some experts say that it is not a bow at all but a whistle and that the creature is blowing down it. But even if this is accepted it opens up the more fascinating idea that Cro-Magnon Man was familiar with flutes.

As a matter of fact, he probably was. Bones have been found, as much as 60,000 years old, hollowed out and capable of producing a musical note if blown across the top. And similar ones with a 'fipple' (stopper) of clay pushed into one end to narrow the wind hole to give a better sound have been dated at 30,000 years ago. And round about the time of Cro-Magnon Man there were hollow bones with three holes drilled in the side to vary the note. Possibly these whistles were used for making hunting signals.

But it is certain that by this period music of a sort had been in existence a long time, perhaps thousands of years. Not music in the way we know it, but sounds produced by twanging bow strings, blowing down hollow bones and beating tree trunks. Perhaps these were used for ceremonial activities, perhaps they were just made for fun.

But without any doubt at all music had arrived.

A prehistoric family relaxing by painting and playing primitive instruments

3 The First Musical Instruments

One of the more surprising things about early man is that he managed to travel so widely. Not in the modern sense of one man going on a long journey and eventually coming back home, but in the fact that fossilized remains millions of years old, in much the same stage of development, have been found in many widely separated places.

There are two different reasons for this. The first is that man's evolution from the animal state probably proceeded at more or less the same rate anywhere in the world where climatic conditions encouraged it. 'More or less the same rate' in this case covering variations of millions of years.

The second reason is that, driven by the ever-changing climatic conditions of the period, man moved further and further afield in search of food. Once he moved, he might as well keep going, since he had no home to go back to. In those times, too, many of the world's great land masses were joined together – there was no English Channel, for instance, until a mere 70,000 years ago – and there were no sea barriers to prevent prehistoric man travelling on and on. The population of the world in those days was so small that it is improbable that our wandering early man met any of his kind wherever he went. In the fairly unlikely event of him running into

When wandering tribes of early men met

another wandering group from another part also engaged in the endless search for food, it is safe to assume that they did not sit down to exchange musical ideas.

But if they had – if they had any musical ideas to discuss – they would have found that they were much the same, since they would be springing from man's basic primitive instincts. It would have been many hundreds of thousands of years before local differences began to take root and grow.

The primitive instruments, and rudimentary musical ideas, described in the previous chapters probably were to be found in much the same stage of development in all parts of the inhabited globe, as mankind evolved from the food-gatherer to the hunter to the farmer. It was only when he began to settle into communities that he began to grow local characteristics.

And so it was, no doubt, with music. At first, the music – if we can call it such – was probably much the same all over the world. Then local differences began to grow up and take a hold, so that, thousands of years later, the music of Europe and India and China was so different that it was hard to believe that it came from a common origin.

The inhabitants of what we now call India, six or seven thousand years ago, were a race of Asiatic pygmies, now extinct. India was then invaded by a dark-skinned race of people called Dravidians, who are thought to have had some relationship with the Australian aborigines. Nothing much is known of the musical attributes of these people except that they associated music with their religions and believed that each note represented an animal cry. The next wave of invasion came from the direction of Egypt, a light-skinned people who brought with them their own musical ideas, including instruments like the reed flute, which eventually evolved into the so-called snake-charmer's pipe, also various kinds of drum.

China five thousand years ago was populated by wandering and hunting tribes, who eventually developed into farmers in the fertile river regions. It is not until about 2000 BC that there is any reliable evidence as to what their music was like. Excavations have revealed a shaped stone which gave out a note when struck, and a flute shaped like a ball. Later there were references to a bell and a drum in a Book of Songs compiled about 1200 BC.

Choirs of boys and girls from various villages would sing in competition; this alternate singing of two choirs (antiphon) we shall meet centuries later in European church music, but there is no evidence that one was copied from the other.

One of the most interesting points about Chinese music is that it has been from time immemorial based on a five-note scale, and still is today. According to one theory this five-note scale was spread over Europe and Asia and was not replaced until Europe developed its own musical culture, leaving it only in the fringe areas like Lapland and the Hebrides and China itself.

4 The Music of Ancient Persia

It took five thousand years for the revolutionary idea of growing food, instead of catching it, to alter man's way of life for good.

He began to settle into communities instead of incessantly wandering, and he did this where the earth was green and fertile and things grew readily – in the great river basins of the world.

From these primitive settlements came communities large enough to be called cities. Thousands of people lived in them; too many for all of them to be occupied in the tasks of growing food and tending the herds of goats, pigs, sheep and cattle, which had also become commonplace by then. So other jobs began to evolve such as weaving, metal working (the casting of copper first appeared in the Nile Valley about 3000 BC and had a vital effect on the development of musical instruments), buying and selling, organised government and religious activities.

One of the greatest of these cities was Susa, the capital of the Sumerians, who occupied what we later called Persia (now Iran). Another was Babylon, capital of the Babylonians (Iraq). Another was Nineveh, capital of the Assyrians (Iraq).

From these cities came many musical instruments and musical ideas. Drums, tambourines and rattles have been dug up, as well as harps of various kinds, lutes (the true ancestor of the modern guitar), curved and straight trumpets of metal, and lyres.

Engravings on walls and pillars show musicians playing flutes, horns, oboes and stringed instruments played with a bow.

In Babylon, professional musicians sang and played at feasts and celebrations. On ancient pottery from Egypt are pictures of workers dancing and singing in the fields – an early example, perhaps, of the 'work songs' which help the monotony of labour. Other pictures show musical instruments being used at harvest time.

16

In many cases the musicians are girls; certain instruments, such as the double-pipe shawm, an early wind instrument, being thought unworthy of masculine attention.

The horn, which was to become a basic instrument of the orchestra, was beginning to evolve. At first it was what the name implied – an animal's horn, hollowed out and curved. It was played without a mouthpiece, the player having to adjust his lips to make what modern brass-instrument players call an 'embouchure' – that is, pursing the lips tightly so that they vibrate when air is forced through them. With-

A group of Babylonian musicians

out doing this a brass instrument will not 'speak' – which explains why many people, blowing a brass instrument for the first time, can get no sound at all.

This was quite a problem for those far-distant horn players and relics have been found that suggest they tried to carve the small end of the horn into a rough mouthpiece to help.

The discovery of copper and then later bronze (a mixture of copper and tin) was to solve the early horn player's problem. Initially, he used it to decorate the outside of the animal horn. Later the idea occurred to him to make the whole

instrument of metal. At first the mouthpiece was built into the instrument, later it became detachable, as it is today.

The earliest instruments made of metal copied the shape of the animal horn. In Scandinavia, great curved bronze trumpets called 'lurs' have been dug up which closely resemble the horns of the mammoth which was known to inhabit those parts.

But very soon the ancient Persian and Egyptian musicians started to experiment with instruments of a greater length and narrower bore, resulting in altogether new and much more brilliant sounds. Even though they were much improved, these early trumpets and horns were very limited musically. They could only play a few notes spaced some distance apart, and their tone was so harsh that they were said to resemble the braying of an ass.

The harp also dates back to Sumerian times. At first with only two strings, it was a simple device rather like an archer's bow (from which it no doubt evolved) with a soundbox at one end to amplify the sound. Two thousand years later the arched harp, as it is called, had developed into the angular harp (shaped like a triangle with one side missing) with as many as ten strings. The arched harp, presumably because it was so much simpler, gradually fell into disfavour until, by Egyptian times, it was played only by beggars.

Another extremely ancient instrument from this distant period is the lute, rather similar in appearance to the early arched harp but with the important difference that whereas the strings of the harp were free, those of the lute could be pressed against a fingerboard, thus enabling the pitch of the note to be changed.

The lyre, also from this period, is a form of small harp, but has two upright sidepieces set into a soundbox with a crossbar at the top from which the strings are stretched to the soundbox.

Although we know quite a lot about the instruments of the period, and how and when music was used, we know nothing at all about the music itself, except by guessing at the sounds produced by the various instruments. There were only simple tunes, played by individual performers or groups. The horns and trumpets, because of their limited range of notes, were used only for signals and fanfares.

5 Music of the Bible

About two thousand years before the birth of Christ, various tribes lived in the desert east of the Mediterranean – in the area that we now call Iraq and Syria. They were wandering shepherds, scraping a living from the bare arid land and moving from place to place in the hope of better feeding for their flocks.

But even in this sparse life they had music – mostly songs aimed at making easier and more tolerable the hard facts of their life. Even today, the Bedouins that inhabit that area have a song *Spring, O Water, Flow in Plenty*.

One of these wandering tribes were the Jews who, first under Abraham, and later Jacob, moved towards the richer lands of Egypt. They were absorbed into the Egyptian way of life, eventually becoming slaves, until Moses led them out of bondage hundreds of years later.

During their stay they picked up a great deal of Egyptian culture, particularly music in the shape of singing, dancing and the playing of instruments. When they eventually settled in the Promised Land (Palestine) and began to build their cities and temples, they had a rich background on which to draw.

Their instruments were a drum, rather like a tambourine (a 'timbrel'), the lyre (a small harp-like instrument), and the flute, blown from the end, rather like the popular school instrument, the recorder.

These were the instruments of the wandering tribesmen, simple to make and simple to play. Only the lyre was probably borrowed from the more advanced Egyptian culture. Another instrument that could have come from the Egyptians was the jingles or bells, which the priests wore attached to their clothes.

For ceremonial purposes they used the ram's horn, called the 'shofar', and a loud metal trumpet used mostly for what we would call fanfares, or signals. It was a blast on these trumpets that was supposed to have brought down the walls of Jericho.

An illuminated page of the Book of Numbers *which contains instructions for the musicians of the tabernacle*

The Book of Genesis mentions two descendants of Cain – Tubal, the worker in brass and iron, who is said to have invented the timbrel (drum), and Jubal, 'the father of all those who play the flute and the lyre.'

The Jews were very skilled in music, using it extensively in their religious ceremonies and festivities. Nor were they averse to picking up ideas and instruments from their neighbours, which gave them a lively and inventive musical culture. When Solomon married Pharaoh's daughter, the tremendous preparations for the event included the ordering of large quantities

18

of specially-made instruments from Egypt.

Under King Saul the Jews became a large and prosperous nation, with its capital in Jerusalem. Vocal music played an ever increasingly important part in court life, as it did in other royal courts of the time. Coronations and their anniversaries, marriages of important courtiers, the departure to and return from wars, were all celebrated with specially written psalms (the word 'psalm' means a hymn accompanied by string instruments).

The *Book of Psalms* of the Bible is the oldest song book still in use. There are 150 Psalms, about half of them written by King David himself, according to some authorities. David was himself a very skilled musician, writing music, singing and performing on the lyre and other instruments, some of which he is said to have invented.

The First Book of *Chronicles* tells us how very carefully the music of the Temple was to be organised. There were to be seventeen singers, three cymbal players, eight psalterers (probably harp players), six harp players (meaning lyres, the words having changed their meanings over centuries of translations), and seven priests to blow the trumpets. It must have been a glorious noise! It also says that the chief Levite was to be songmaster 'because he was wise'.

Despite all this detail about the way music was to be performed, we unfortunately have no way of telling how it sounded as there was no written music. All we can guess is that the tunes were based on the words of the songs – that is, with the same accents. The tunes themselves were probably little more than the alternation of two or three notes, because of the limitations of the instruments themselves. It is very unlikely that there was any attempt at harmony.

Nevertheless, despite its primitive form, music was a very important part of Biblical people and their times.

Hebrew musicians performing before King David with harps, cymbals and trumpets

6 Theory and Practice

The Greeks excelled in many things – art, architecture, philosophy, government, mathematics – and they brought to music all their high intelligence and creative powers. They invented patterns of music called 'modes' which were the forerunners of our system of keys. Their great poems were not spoken but sung or chanted. The Greeks even gave us the word 'music', meaning 'belonging to the Muses', the goddesses of learning, dancing and astronomy.

For the first time music became something to be listened to for its own sake, instead of being just an accompaniment for religion, work, wars or ceremonies. Individual musicians attained great skill and became stars, just like the pop singers of today, to be admired, applauded and richly rewarded.

Their instruments were the flute, the trumpet and the usual percussion instruments, all of which we have met before. In addition, they had the 'aulos', an instrument consisting of two separate pipes, joined together at the blowing end, and each fingered by one hand. Another important instrument was the 'kithara', which consisted of 3 to 12 strings stretched from a sound

A group of Greek kithara players waiting to perform at a banquet in the 5th century BC

box to a cross arm supported by two curved necks. A simpler version of this, used by the non-professionals, was the 'lyra'.

Also used by the amateurs were the panpipes or 'syrinx', made from a number of pipes joined together in a straight line and played by moving it across the mouth, just like the modern mouth-organ, or harmonica. Another instrument was the 'lute', which had a long neck and a rounded body, rather like the guitar of today.

The ancient Greeks were formed, as were most of the nations of that time, by the combining of wandering tribes from Europe and what we would call the Middle East. The tribes had different names and these names were given to the five different modes, or 'patterns' of music – the Lydian, Phrygian, Dorian, Aeolian and Ionian. Composers of ancient Greece used the five different patterns on which to build various kinds of tunes. Classical Greek music consisted of five types of tunes: hymns, dirges, songs of victory, songs of revelry, songs for instruments – and each kept closely to its own particular

mode. These modes survive to this day and are still used in the more technical aspects of writing music.

The ancient Greeks were great thinkers and theorists, and the art of music did not escape the attention of their scholars. The great mathematician Pythagoras, who lived five hundred years before the birth of Christ, reduced the whole thing to a system of numbers, designed to improve the spirit and uplift the soul. The skies and the stars were imagined as a kind of 'harmony' and a single stretched string was used to illustrate the 'divine harmony of the spheres'. Tireless in their experiments, Pythagoras and his friends compiled a huge amount of analyses of intervals and sounds, covering all the intervals known to modern music and many more besides. The geometrician Euclid, two hundred years later, also added much to musical theory, as did the philosopher Plato.

The ordinary Greek musician took very little heed of all this theorising, preferring to trust his ears rather than his uncertain grasp of mathematics. In one way this was a pity, for the mathematicians had laid down the basic principles of harmony which still prevail 2,500 years later. But Greek music, despite all its elaboration with instruments and instrumental skill, depended very little on what we understand as harmony; that is, two or more notes of different pitch played simultaneously, which gives music its

true richness.

We know from a few fragments on stone and papyrus that the Greeks had evolved a system of writing music down, though all of them are dated about 200 BC and not one is complete. Thus, once again, we know a great deal about how the music was performed and how it was regarded, but almost nothing of how it sounded.

Preparing wine for the Feast of Dionysius accompanied (right) by a player on the double-aulos

Two musicians from the Chinese Imperial Court

7 Eastern Music

The Chinese have a remarkable legend about music. The story is that a certain Emperor, who is said to have lived three thousand years before the birth of Christ, sent his Music Ruler to a certain valley at the outer rim of his kingdom where grew a bamboo tree of magical significance. When he found this he was to cut off a length of bamboo which, when blown, sounded the 'perfect note', representing the pitch of a man's voice when he spoke without undue anger or joy.

This 'perfect note' tube of bamboo was then to provide the basis of a second tube, two-thirds the length of the first; then a tube one-third longer than the second, and so on. From this system, the Chinese five-note scale was evolved.

Thousands of years later this system had evolved into eighty-four different modes or scales, and an Imperial Office of Music was established, attached to the Office of Weights and Measures. Orchestras contained as many as eight hundred performers, and there were over two hundred different instruments, among them the

23

stone-chime (a series of different-sized stone plates hung in a frame), a bell-chime (twenty-four metal bells suspended in a frame), a reed mouth organ consisting of a dozen or so bamboo pipes bound together and fastened to a gourd with a mouthpiece, flutes, gongs, cymbals, triangles, miscellaneous drums, and the zither (a box-like instrument with strings stretched across it).

There was no harmony except the simplest. Chinese music depended on the inflexions and tones given to each individual note and the balances of sound qualities of the various instruments. To obscure these delicate nuances by adding complex Western-style harmony would have seemed crude.

Visitors from foreign lands brought new instruments (the Persian harp) and new styles of music from India, Turkey and Tibet. By the twentieth century, Western-style music had begun to penetrate, and China today has symphony orchestras on European lines and has produced pianists and violinists of international virtuoso level.

But not all the traffic has been one way. In the eighteenth century the Chinese mouth organ was introduced into Russia and its 'free reed' (which is fixed at one end only) was introduced into Europe by a German organ builder. The modern accordion is its direct descendant, as is the harmonium and Larry Adler's harmonica. Weber's overture to the play *Turandot*, makes use of the Chinese five-note scale.

In India a seven-note scale is used, as in Western music. But there the similarity ends, for the Indian scale is further divided into twenty-two steps each fractionally less than a quarter-tone. These are grouped together according to complicated rules to produce *ragas*, which are music shapes that express different emotions and thoughts. There is said to be a different *raga* for every hour, season, day of the week, colour, sex, temperament, zodiacal sign and so on. There were 12,000 different ones among the ancient people of India, and there was trouble if anyone sang the wrong one at the wrong moment. This called for a pretty considerable feat of memory, if nothing else. Today, these *ragas* still exist, but their number has been cut down to a usable sixty or so.

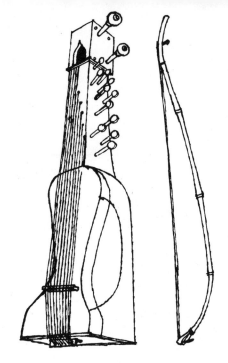

A sarangi, a multi-stringed instrument from North India, played with a bow

To these *raga* note patterns are added rhythmic time-measures, called *talas*, and the combined *raga* and *tala* is then completed by a *kharaja*, or droning note, like the bagpipe sound. This is played on an Indian version of the lute, the strings being struck without any regard to the rhythmic structure of the piece, so that a continuous wave of sound is produced.

This is extremely complicated and sounds very strange to Western ears. As with Chinese music, no harmony is added, it being considered that to do so would obscure the inner beauties of what is already there.

Pieces composed on the *raga-tala-kharaja* framework have no definite starting or finishing point, and can last anything from twenty minutes to an hour-and-a-half.

Indian music, because it is an extemporisation by the performer, is not written down. There have been attempts to evolve a method of notation but these are of little value, because the works are performed differently every time they are played.

Indian music has had a considerable effect on the music of other Eastern countries such as China and Japan and the *tala-raga* system existed long before a similar system arose in Persia. European composers like Gustav Holst have incorporated certain aspects of Indian music into their works.

Some of it reached Europe through the

gypsies, an Aryan people who originated in India and travelled the world in the past, bringing with them certain *ragas* and instruments such as the cymbalum.

But the best known Indian instrument is the 'sitar', made familiar by the virtuoso performances of Ravi Shankar and others on visits to Europe and America. This instrument, which looks like a fantastically complicated guitar, is really a combination of the Persian lute and the Indian 'vina', or zither. Attempts have been made to introduce the sitar into the beat groups, but without much success. Its technique is extremely difficult and takes a lifetime of study to master.

One of the more surprising items of Indian music, bearing in mind how very different it is from Western music, is the adoption of the violin, introduced into India by the British in the late eighteenth century. The violin, because it does not have stops and keys, lends itself very readily to the quarter-tones and subtle tunings of Indian music, especially after its Europeanised tuning has been changed to fit Indian ideas.

Ravi Shankar, Indian
virtuoso of the sitar

8 Praise Him With Music

There is no doubt that one of the most powerful influences in the whole history of music has been the Church. This applies to the churches of all countries and religions.

There seems always to have been a strong affinity between music and religion. The power and influence of religious authority has provided not only an immense impetus to the development of music, but a living for countless thousands of composers, teachers and performers. Indeed, it is safe to say that without the Church, music would not be where it is today.

But for the value given there was also value received. The beauty and impressiveness of most church services would be considerably less were it not for the music that accompanies them.

If we go back five or six thousand years to the early civilisations of Mesopotamia, we find stepped towers called 'ziggurats' in which the people worshipped their gods with words and music. Their thunder god was Ramman, who destroyed their crops and had to be placated with music—the sound of their reed pipes was likened to Ramman's breath; and their name for a drum was written with the word for Ea, another god who was apt to flood their lands if they misbehaved.

Those times are too distant for us to know much about them except from laboriously deciphered writings on fragments of pottery and buildings. But almost certainly these musico-religious ideas were old even then and came from even earlier times. By 4000 BC the Sumerians had developed alternate singing of hymns or psalms by priest and choir, and what was to be known thousands of years later as 'antiphon', or alternate singing by two choirs.

The Babylonians, two thousand years later, made music even more important in their religious services, which included over twenty psalms and hymns in each service. There were two main sorts of song used: the 'ershemma' or song of the flute and the 'kishub' or song of prostration. Every god had a special series of these, which were addressed exclusively to him. There was also a private ritual involving only one priest and one layman who sang alternately. They also introduced women singers into the temple choirs.

Daniel in the Old Testament (Daniel III 5) describes in great detail the musical arrangements ordered by the Assyrian king Nebuchadnezzar (600 BC) for the dedication of a new golden image he had installed:

'That at what time ye hear the sound of the cornet (probably horn), flute (reed pipes), harp (lyre), sackbut (early trombone), psaltery (low soundbox harp), dulcimer (high soundbox harp), and all kinds of music (the full orchestra) ye fall down and worship the golden image that Nebuchadnezzar the king hath set up.'

The Jews were exceptionally devoted to music. At the dedication of King Solomon's temple a hundred and twenty priests blew trumpets and two hundred and forty-eight Levites (men of the tribe of Levi, specially appointed by King David to look after the music of the temples) sang and sounded their instruments '. . . in praising and thanking the Lord.'

Throughout the Old Testament there are many references to music. In the early parts the references are mostly to work songs and celebrations, but later it is clear that music had

12th century choir singing Mass in a monastery

become an essential part of worship – 'It is good to sing praises unto the Lord.' St Paul told the Ephesians and Colossians to use music with their worship in hymns and psalms.

Music grew in religious importance in the first three or four hundred years after Christ. Hebrew and Greek elements were all mixed up together, together with influences from the Arabian world and even further afield.

But while the use of music was growing in the church it was also growing outside the church; for festivals, and meetings and celebrations, wars and births and marriages. Songs were being written and instruments developed. There were, in fact, two kinds of music growing up side by side: one for the purposes of worship and one for life outside the church.

The latter was less controlled, more vigorous. Some of the words of the songs were vulgar and so were some of the occasions at which they were used.

The effect of this on the church was important. At one time music was shunned as being too closely associated with evil things, and for a while it was forbidden in the churches. But apart from the fact that the people liked to have music with their religion, there were good reasons why religious services should be chanted. In a large building, chanted words are clearer than spoken words. It is also more solemn and important-sounding. So music was taken back into the church, but without instruments.

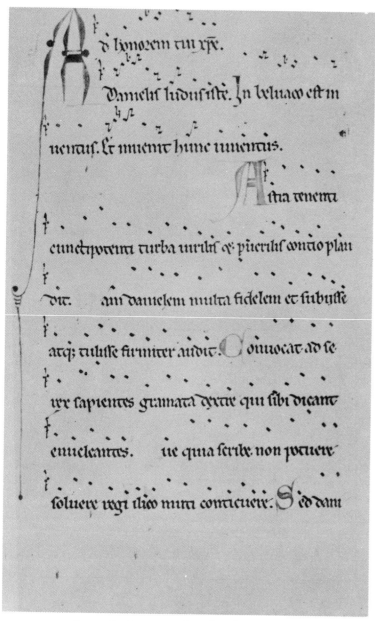

*An ancient manuscript showing
neumes to denote the shape of the tune*

This chanting became an essential part of church music and from it grew what is called 'plainsong', still used today. It is a simple form of music, based on the rhythms of speech rather than on musical requirements. It contains no harmony or ornamentation since it was thought that any such decoration might obscure the words, which were regarded as far more important than the tune. There is very little tune in the modern sense.

Most plainsong was written between the fifth and eighth centuries but at that time there was no way of committing them to paper, so they were handed down from teacher to choir for many centuries. As may be imagined, this led to many variations, with extra bits, even extra versions, being added. The earliest plainsong manuscripts date from the ninth century, but are not much help as they have no indication of pitch.

The desire to get church music organised led two early churchmen, St. Ambrose in the fourth century and Pope Gregory in the sixth century, to make strenuous efforts to get it under control. It also led to something far more important musically; the invention of a way of writing down music so that anyone could read it without having to be taught the tune, as is told in a later chapter.

St. Ambrose was Bishop of Milan and a powerful figure in the politics of the time. He seems to have been responsible for organising the chanting of psalms and other parts of the liturgy into a firm system with set rules. He introduced the singing of antiphons (two choirs singing alternately); probably getting the idea from Greece. He also started the practice of singing hymns as opposed to the chanting of psalms during services.

Pope St. Gregory was an important figure in the history of church music. Not only did he bring order into what had grown into a sprawling and disorganised mountain of religious music, but he was also a considerable writer of chants himself.

He reorganised the School of Singing in Rome, from which pupils were sent all over the world to teach the Gregorian chants.

Gregory's reputation as a writer of music has been illustrated in paintings of the period which show him sitting on the papal throne, dictating to a faithful scribe the melodies that a heavenly dove is whispering into his ear.

St. Augustine of Canterbury, who was sent by Gregory to England as his personal representative, brought with him the authorised liturgies (church services) and chants and laid down that these and these only were to be used in all religious festivities. That was in AD 597 and one hundred and fifty years later, in AD 747, the Council of Cloveshoe (Glasgow) sharply reminded all English churches that they must not depart from the plainsong chant book brought from Rome.

By the year AD 800 composers of church music had hardly any work to do, so frozen was the pattern of Gregorian chant or plainsong. So they began to take the odd word – such as 'Hallelu' (Praise ye), and embellish it to such an extent that these shouts of praise from the old Jewish church began to grow into complete works for choir and soloist. These works were banned from the church service proper but they were used for religious processions at Easter and Christmas and eventually grew into the 'miracle plays' of the eleventh century.

But all this musical inventing and exploring was not always popular with church dignitaries. In the fourteenth century, Pope John XXII forbade the use of secular (non-religious) music in church services. It had become the practice to borrow the catchy melodies that were being sung in the taverns and danced to on the village greens, and set religious words to them.

Many centuries later, General Booth, the head of the Salvation Army, took an entirely opposite view and encouraged the Army bands to adapt the popular hits of the day as hymns, saying that he 'didn't see why the devil should have all the good tunes.'

A 10th century organ, with two sets of blowers and two players

Group of strolling minstrels entertaining the lord and lady with harp, rebec and bagpipes

9 Minstrels and Troubadours

Telling stories in song is not new. Indeed, it has been going on almost as long as mankind itself. As far back as we can trace man has entertained himself and his friends by telling stories; of adventure, of conquest, of love, of happiness, of disaster; and it seems to have been an instinct that these stories sounded better with music.

This is not to say that 'story songs' suddenly sprang into existence, words and music all complete and neatly rounded off. The earliest forms leaned far more heavily on words rather than music. The latter was either a simple chant, the tune consisting of only a few simple notes; or a simple musical phrase tacked on the end of a large number of spoken words.

In the Middle Ages, the thousand years or so from the fall of the Roman Empire in about the fifth century AD to the great flowering of man's intellect in the fifteenth century, the story song reached its peak in the hands of the wandering performers. They were mostly men of little education but much talent who made a living going from town to town, from castle to castle; entertaining with acrobatics, juggling, dancing, singing, playing instruments; in fact, a touring road show. They had no regular theatres, usually they performed in the open in the village square. If they were better than average they got invited into the homes of the local nobility and perhaps stayed there for several days before moving on to the next place.

Sometimes they became permanently attached to the households of the barons and lords, who used them to entertain not only themselves but their tenants.

These were minstrels. They accompanied themselves on simple instruments like the 'crwth' (pronounced crooth, a kind of square box with strings across it played with a bow, a very primitive forerunner of the violin), the 'rebec' (a small guitar-shaped instrument also played with a bow), and a hurdy-gurdy, which was a string instrument rather like a fat violin but played by turning a handle.

When William of Normandy landed at Hastings in 1066, it was his minstrel who led the Normans into the battle against King Harold, singing part of the *Chanson de Roland*, an early French epic.

There were also at this time travelling students who moved about seeking new masters to support them. They were better educated than the minstrels but also used song as part of their stock-in-trade. They were young, poor and high spirited, and their songs reflected their characters. They were called 'goliards', after a mythical Bishop Golias, who was over fond of wine, women and song.

The blend of the minstrels and the goliards eventually produced the 'troubadour', an educated, high-born, amateur singer-writer-composer. They came from the lords and barons, who listened to the travelling professional minstrels, thought they could do better and joined in. Eventually some of them became so fascinated with the art that they devoted all their time to it.

To begin with, the amateur used to write the words and have the minstrel merely add a few notes of music. Some of these poems were immensely long, perhaps a thousand lines, with the same few notes repeated over and over again at the end of each verse.

These troubadours performed mostly in the southern part of France, but their counterparts, known as 'trouvères' were to be found in the north of France. The troubadours concentrated very heavily upon love poetry and built up a very complicated code of behaviour for approaching and wooing their lady loves. Much of the chivalry in the stories of King Arthur and his knights comes from them. The trouvères were very much influenced by the troubadours but they also took much from the earlier epics and stories of adventure; their poetry had far more action in it. In Germany they were called 'minnesingers' (love singers) and the best of them formed themselves into Guilds of Mastersingers, eventually to be the subject of an opera by Richard Wagner, *The Mastersingers of Nuremberg*, many hundreds of years later.

Blondin, most famous of all the minstrels, searches for the imprisoned King Richard

These singers, both amateur and professional, were a great influence on the culture of the Middle Ages. Apart from establishing standards of romantic honour, they encouraged a sense of responsibility in their songs of great deeds by great princes, the protection of the weak, the vanquishing of the wicked, and the upholding of the standards of chivalry.

The first known troubadour was William, Count of Poitiers, who lived at the end of the eleventh century. But the most famous was Richard Coeur de Lion, King of England from 1189 to his death in 1199. Richard had a minstrel, Blondin, who was his master's right-hand man in things more important than music.

Thibaut, King of Navarre, was another royal trouvère. The strolling minstrel, Colin Muset, became famous throughout Europe. The skills of minstrelsy and the educated art of the troubadours and trouvères spread through Spain, Italy and Germany. Oddly enough, England does not seem to have been much touched by this form of music, apart from King Richard and his faithful Blondin.

The earliest troubadours did not write their own melodies but borrowed them from the popular music of the times, either dance tunes or hymns; any good tune was good enough to borrow and such things as copyright did not exist. Nor did these tunes have much life outside their own small circle. It was not until much later that the more skilful of the musician-historians of the thirteenth and fourteenth centuries began to compile 'chansonniers' (song books) for their wealthy masters and many of these collections survive to this day.

It was from the work of the troubadours and their like that much of today's music comes. The songs, the ballads and even some of the hymns led to opera in later centuries and the complicated musicalities of the symphony orchestra.

It is sad to have to record that eventually minstrelsy became such a popular way of earning a living that by Elizabethan times there was an over-abundance of wandering players. The result was that they were officially branded as 'rogues and vagabonds', having no civil rights and liable to arrest and imprisonment for no other reason than that they sang for their suppers and had no other means of support.

10 The First Writing of Music

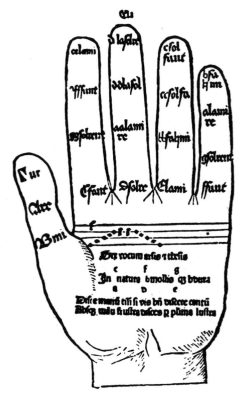

The Guidonian Hand – 11th century way of teaching music

With music playing a greater and greater role in men's lives it soon became necessary to find some way of writing it down. This might seem obvious now but just imagine the problems it presented then.

Someone would create a good tune. Perhaps he would remember it, perhaps not. If not, a good tune was lost for ever. Or a churchman would write a hymn and the choirmaster set it to a tune for the choir to sing. Later there would be new choirboys, even a new choirmaster, who did not know the tune, and it would upset the church service until a new tune was found and learned.

So, many attempts were made to find a written system to instruct the singers what the tune was. At first this was done by placing little marks over the words to show whether the notes went up or down. These were called 'neumes' and gave the singer a rough idea of what to do – but only a rough idea.

The ancient Greeks had had a system of using letters to indicate certain notes, as had the Romans. But these were used more for scientific discussion by Pythagoras and his friends when they were working out the note patterns or 'modes' on which Greek music was based.

Early church music used the Greek modes as the foundation of its chants, but over the centuries so much variation and alteration crept in that by the middle of the fourth century AD the Bishop of Milan, St. Ambrose, tried to bring some order in to church music by limiting the use of the Greek modes to four. This served for a while but by the sixth century the great Pope St. Gregory felt that a more rigid system was necessary in order that all church services and their music should have some uniformity and issued strict orders to this effect. As a result, further modes were added and the first serious attempts were made to find a system of writing down music.

By the seventh century the neumes method was well established. It was, however, very primitive, consisting of little more than grave (indicating lowering) and acute (indicating raising) accents placed over the words and served merely to remind the singer of the tune which he already had learned by hearing others sing or play it.

A medieval lute

Gradually these neumes became more and more elaborate. First, they began to be spaced out to give a clearer idea of the rise and fall of the notes. Later the actual neumes themselves were written higher or lower, following an imaginary line. Then the actual line was added thus making the first true start on music writing as we know it today, the stave.

Then the line was drawn in red. Then in a great advance, two lines were used. This proved to be such a great help that it was not very long before still more lines were added until a total of four became fairly well fixed and remains in use today for certain kinds of church music called 'plainsong'. Eventually, for other kinds of music a fifth line was added and so was born the 'five-line stave' used throughout the Western world today.

But the writers of those distant days, nearly a thousand years ago, did not know how important their work was and how it was to last into a future they could not even imagine. They treated their own invention with scant respect, adding or taking away lines just as the mood took them. It was considered a great waste of effort to have lines which were not actually needed for notes. Not only a waste of effort in drawing the unnecessary lines, but what was perhaps more important, a waste of valuable parchment.

Although the stave showed the pitch of the notes, it did not say anything about their duration. It was not until well into the tenth century that any attempt was made to show how long each note should be sung or played. Different shapes were used; heavy black squares, diamonds and oblongs. The shortest note then in use was called a 'semibreve' (it is now the longest), then came the 'breve', and finally the 'long', which just to make things more complicated, changed its value according to where it was placed.

As you may imagine, reading music was a difficult business and those who suffered most were the choirboys.

One of the ways of teaching them was with an instrument called a 'monochord' (one string), a single wire stretched across a sound box with a moveable bridge supporting it. The names of the notes were written on the sound box and the bridge moved to the appropriate spot and the string plucked. A pretty slow process, one would imagine, but the monk who devised this gadget claimed that with its use he could train choirboys to sight-read in a week.

An eleventh-century book gives us another reason why they learned so quickly. 'If the boys commit any fault either by sleeping or such like transgressions,' it says, 'let them be stripped forthwith of frock and cowl and beaten in their shirt only, with pliant and smooth osier rods provided for that special purpose.'

But a better idea was on its way. Guido of Arezzo (born about 995) a French-born Italian monk, was the greatest teacher of music of his time and came to the rescue of the sorely-tried choirboys by inventing a series of six syllables to match the different notes. He called it 'solmization' and used the syllables 'ut, re, mi, fa, sol, la' (which were the first syllables of each line of a hymn in Latin which every choirboy knew); he also coloured the spaces where the semitones occurred red or yellow. Some eight hundred years later in the 1840's, a Congregation minister named John Curwen updated the system to 'doh, ray, me, fah, soh, lah, te, doh' and called it 'Tonic Sol-fa'. This system is widely used today in schools and by choirs as a very easy way of teaching 'sight singing'—that is, singing instantly and correctly at first sight a completely unknown piece of music.

Wrote Guido: 'If anyone doubt (the value of the system) let him come and hear what small boys can do under our direction, boys who have until now been beaten for their gross ignorance of the psalms.'

So should any choirboys be reading this, let them offer up a silent prayer of thanks to that long-dead monk of Northern Italy, Guido of Arezzo.

LEFT: *Guido of Arezzo demonstrates the monochord to Theobaldus. It was used for teaching pitch to choirs*

11 The Oldest Written Music

What is the oldest piece of written music? Unfortunately, the question cannot be answered with any certainty. There are so many claimants and we have no way of deciding which has the best claim.

One possible claimant might be the clay tablet of Sumerian times, found in Iraq a few years ago, which bears what has been deciphered as an eight-note scale, and which dates back to 1800 BC – nearly four thousand years ago.

Then there are other fragments – two stone carvings, six pieces of papyrus and some textbooks – from ancient Greece, dating back some two thousand years.

There is a Greek manuscript of the third century written in 'alphabet notation' – that is, with some of the letters of the alphabet indicating various notes, but without any pitch, or intervals, or time.

There are Spanish manuscripts of the eighth century of Moslem-Arabic chants, and several pages of beautifully-copied parchment in a Swiss monastery from the same period.

There are many descriptions of music and writings on the theory of the subject, and it is from these that we get a glimmering of what music of the past was like.

There are a number of manuscripts with neumes, including the Swiss ones mentioned above, but these were not true music manuscripts as we understand the word today and give only a very vague idea of the tunes.

Even Hucbald, a Franco-Flemish monk of the tenth century, who did a great deal towards simplifying and clarifying the system when he cut down the three hundred signs handed down by the Greeks and Romans to a handlable fifteen, was not very enthusiastic about the system, for he wrote: 'The first note seems to be higher; you can sing it wherever you like. The second you can see is lower, but when you try to join it to the first you cannot decide whether the interval is one, two, or three tones. Unless you hear it sung you cannot tell what the composer intended.'

So even though there are examples of Hucbald's work, using letters of the alphabet to help fix the pitch, it is a matter of opinion whether they rate as the oldest music manuscripts.

But Hucbald did something else; he began to establish harmony, which he described as 'two notes, entirely different in pitch, which are sounded together.' The requirements of harmony demanded two things: the extra lines which were to build up the stave as we know it today, and the giving of time values to the notes.

During this period of the tenth to the twelfth centuries, a large amount of music was written, showing the slow evolution of the system as we know it. Some of these manuscripts can still be seen in museums today, many in the form of large volumes too heavy to hold. The monks used to stand round these huge books, which were placed on a stand in the middle of the Sacristy, reading the music of the hymns – one wonders how those who were standing on the outer edge of the group managed to see, since the manuscript was not very legible in any case.

The monasteries where these manuscripts were written maintained scores of monk-copyists to do the job, who used to write comments in the margins such as 'The tedious plainsong grates my tender ears.' A somewhat crusty individual, one imagines, going about with a sour face and his teeth set firmly on edge; not at all like another monk who wrote joyously in the margin of his manuscript 'Nightfall and time for supper.'

Probably among these works must come the oldest piece of written music, but nobody knows which it is.

The Cathedral Library of Compostela contains a fine collection of twelfth century music manuscripts – pilgrim songs, plainsongs, religious pieces and even some three-part harmony.

One of the most interesting pieces of early manuscript is that of a song called *Sumer is i-cumen in* (Summer Is Coming In) which dates from the early thirteenth century. It is specially interesting for several reasons – the tune is still sung today and can be bought in modern notation for a few shillings, and the original

The original manuscript of Sumer Is a-Cumin In

BELOW: *An early bowed instrument, the rebec*

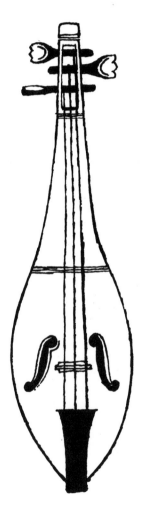

manuscript is in the British Museum for anyone to go and look at.

But even more interesting is that it is at least a century ahead of its time in the complexity of its writing. At this time harmony was of the simplest, but *Sumer* is written for four voices, with two bass tunes underneath—a most involved kind of six-part writing, quite astonishing for its age.

It is a 'round': that is, a work in which the tune is interwoven with other parts of the same tune in a kind of echo effect, each part picking up from the other, the tune going round, in fact.

Some say that it was written by John of Fornsete, a monk of Reading Abbey, from hearing it performed at a spring festival. Whether this is true or not, it is certainly the oldest composition for six voices.

12 To the Glory of God

The term 'Middle Ages' is a rather loose one and tends to have various meanings according to the subject being discussed.

In the study of history it is usually taken to mean the thousand years between the fall of the Western Roman Empire in the fifth century to the beginning of the Renaissance in the fifteenth.

For our purposes, however, this is too long a span – too much happened in the realm of music during that thousand years for it to be considered as a single-period. To go in one jump, as it were, from single-line unwritten singing to the complex musical masterpieces of Palestrina and Lassus, covers too much ground.

12th century courtiers playing a shawm, a rebec, a psaltery and a 16-note hand organ

To understand how this came about, it is necessary to go step by step through this long and vitally important period in the development of music.

Up to the fifth century AD religious music had been more or less limited to the chanted parts of church services. Secular (non-religious) music consisted of love songs, work songs, and music for festive occasions played on lyres, lutes, harps, pipes, flutes, trumpets and percussion instruments of various kinds – all of them very primitive and very little like their modern equivalents.

There was no harmony and no written music. When people sang together they all sang the same note; tunes were learned by hearing someone else sing them.

Around the sixth century, a Roman scholar named Cassiodorus showed that it was not necessary for everyone to sing the same note and that a quite pleasing effect could be obtained by singing two notes simultaneously four

39

or five steps apart, as Pythagoras had worked out mathematically hundreds of years previously. This was a vitally important idea and the development of it was perhaps the single most progressive musical happening of the Middle Ages, because it led to polyphony (that is, the sounding of several different notes at once) which is the basis of all modern music.

It was not until the ninth century, however, that this idea really caught on and then it did so more or less by accident.

The accident was that Pope Vitalian, in the seventh century, cautiously allowed the re-introduction of musical instruments into the church. (They had been banned by an earlier Pope on the grounds that they were too vulgar for religious purposes and distracted the worshippers' minds from the seriousness of what was being chanted.)

The instrument chosen for the come back was the organ, not a great majestic instrument such as we know today, but a small affair, capable of being carried in a procession, and having only about ten or twelve pipes. The purpose of allowing this instrument to be used was to aid the choir with its singing and, presumably, to help them keep in tune with one another.

The pitch of the organs was a matter of taste rather than system – some were pitched high and some were pitched low. Mostly they consisted of a single row of pipes, but sometimes they had a double row, pitched four or five notes apart, played by two organists.

It was these last named organs, producing such an agreeable sound when the two rows of pipes were sounded together in duet, that constituted the foundation of singing in harmony. The choirmasters liked the sound of the organs and their singers imitated it. This was called 'organizing,' for obvious reasons, and grew to be so popular that the whole method received a name of its own – 'organum' (accent on the first syllable) and had a far-reaching influence on the development of music, since it was the real foundation of harmony.

It is worth noting, in passing, that Indian and Chinese music never encountered this accident' and therefore never developed harmony.

Once organum was established the idea of harmonizing developed rapidly. Soon, notes other than the fourth and fifth were tried. Next to be added was a third (three notes apart). Then – very daringly – the harmonized note was sung above the melody note, a device that still persists today in pop groups.

The idea caught on like wildfire. There is a treatise of the ninth century that shows how to 'double' the melody line with fourths, fifths, octaves, thirds and twelfths (an octave plus a fifth).

The next startling innovation was to cause the harmony lines to move in opposite directions from the melody line. This was considered very venturesome at the time although today it is an elementary rule in all beginner student's handbooks on harmony.

But new ideas must not stand still: the inflexible rule is Develop or Die. And the new idea of harmony was no exception.

From being simple note-for-note harmonisation, it soon developed into having more than one harmony note to accompany one melody note. This presented no great difficulties when the work was learned by ear. But writing it down presented considerable problems.

Written music had by now developed the stave so at least the pitch was established. Next came note values – essential if one note in the melody was to be held while several notes were to be sounded in the harmony. It soon became necessary to invent yet another device which today we take for granted: the bar line, a line drawn vertically across the stave which groups notes together. The first use of bar lines was in the fourteenth century as a help to the choirmaster, and they did not come into general use until the sixteenth. At first they were merely aids to the eye to keep all the associated notes in one 'box', so to speak, and having no particular duration. It was only later that bar lines came to be the means of making bars of equal value and providing a beat to music.

The other great development was that of 'counterpoint,' without which modern music could not exist. This consists of a combination of simultaneous 'parts' or 'voices,' each being important in itself and the whole blending together in a harmonious texture.

The evolving of polyphony (many sounds) through organum, harmony and counterpoint – and the creation of a clear system of notation (staves, note values, bar lines) were the vitally important contributions to music of the Middle Ages. There were few great musicians and few masterworks in this thousand years – but there were many gifted teachers, scholars and experimenters and a huge amount of choral music that was, in its day, new and venturesome.

One of the types of religious writing which developed as a kind of side issue was the motet (French *mot* = word; motet = small word), in which a separate word was added to every note of the counterpart variation; different words from those being sung to the principle tune, sometimes in a different language.

Thus a three-part motet might have a French love song in the highest part, a Latin prayer to Our Lady in the middle, and a plainsong chant at the bottom – all going on at once!

Strictly speaking, the motet is only for unaccompanied voices but instruments began to creep in and there is a fourteenth century picture showing the kind of group that probably accompanied motet singers – long trumpet, harp, rebec (a primitive sort of fiddle), bent trumpet, portable 16-note organ, and psaltery (a D-shaped flat box with strings across it).

One aspect of music that did not develop in the Middle Ages was orchestral writing and playing. There were several reasons for this – one was that throughout the period the church dominated music and found no place for large groups of instruments which might drown the all-important words; another reason was that orchestral instruments were slow in developing technically – the pipes had few if any keys, only holes, the trumpets had no valves, the viols were weak in tone. The 'families' of instruments were not to be developed until the sixteenth and seventeenth centuries. Finally, because of all these reasons, composers were concentrating on choral music.

There were, to be sure, other instruments than those mentioned above in common use like the 'shawm' (a primitive oboe), recorder, end-blown flute, lute, bagpipes and various drums, bells, jingles and other percussion. But writing for them consisted mostly of embellishments for the voice. The orchestral sound had not yet come into existence.

Many of these instruments were used by the minstrels, troubadours and minnesingers who, towards the end of the Middle Ages, also benefited from the new musical skills of the period, borrowing the most popular of the religious motets and adding their own words. They also hired trained musicians to write tunes in the modern manner for them, until they became skilful enough in musical techniques to write their own 'chansonniers' (song books) for wealthy patrons, many of which are still in existence and some of which can be bought in up-to-date transcriptions together with recordings.

Medieval manuscript showing musicians playing a lute and singing in a garden

13 Organs – Great and Small

One of the most important instruments is the organ. As has been told, the introduction of the organ into church music in the seventh century led to the music form known as 'organum,' and thence to the whole structure of modern harmony, the foundations of which were laid in the Middle Ages.

But the organ was old even in the seventeenth century. It was supposed by legend to have been invented by the god Pan. The story goes that one day he was pursuing a nymph named Syrinx who, not wanting to be caught, appealed to woodland friends to protect her, which they did by turning her into a bundle of reeds. Pan did not know what had happened to her but he heard the wind blowing across the open tops of the reeds, making such a pleasant noise that he gave up the chase and began experimenting with the reeds, binding them together, long ones and short ones, and blowing across the top to make music. The result was called the Pan pipes, or syrinx, after the nymph's name.

Be this as it may, it is true that blowing across the open ends of pipes is a very ancient way indeed of making music and can be traced back to primitive man with his whistles made of hollowed-out finger bones. Who thought of grouping the pipes together is not known but fragments of shepherd's panpipes, or something very like them, have been found dating back thousands of years.

It was left to an ingenious Egyptian, Ktesibos of Alexandria, to invent, in the third century BC, a method of playing the syrinx without all the effort of blowing across them. His device was called a *hydraulus*, (water organ), and had two tanks of water to maintain the air pressure over three octaves of notes, the latter being operated by sliding keys which opened or shut the various pipes. These sliders even operated on groups of pipes, thereby providing what present-day organists call 'mixture stops' – a fantastically advanced idea in those days.

It is said that Nero was delighted with the *hydraulus* and even added refinements to it.

One of its oddities is that it was capable of playing polyphonic (many sounds) music before it was invented and this was considered to be rather a handicap, so that the *hydraulus* was limited to circuses and open-air theatres, where its powerful tone could be heard by everyone present.

But it was very heavy to move about because of all the water and eventually, round about the

42

A baroque organ – the name given to an instrument of the Bach period

nine century, it was supplanted by the wind-blown organ. Although the ancient Greeks and Romans regarded the *hydraulus* as a rather vulgar instrument instrument (like the blaring fairground roundabout organ), as soon as it became windblown it was absorbed into the church. From the time Pope Vitalian introduced it in the seventh century, it became an essential part of worship, and most chroniclers from the ninth century onwards, refer to it in relation to Christian worship.

Initially, these early church organs were small affairs with a dozen or so notes, their bellows pumped by the organist's assistant. Sometimes it was even smaller and carried by the player during processions, one hand finger-ing the keys and the other pumping the miniature bellows.

Then came larger and larger versions, with two men alternately stepping on and stepping off the bellows.

There is a story of a vast organ built at Winchester Abbey in AD 980 which had keys so huge (5 ft 9 ins by 6 ins) that they had to be struck by the clenched fist, or even the foot, to make them operate. It took two men to play it and no less than sixty to pump the bellows. The working of the bellows made so much noise that they had to be placed outside the building.

The creation of polyphony gave a great advantage to the organ, since it was the only instrument that could play several notes simul-taneously. It was reduced to a reasonable size, extra notes and pipes were added to extend its range and, about 1300, a pedal board was added so that the lowest notes could be played by the feet. Later, a second keyboard for the hands was added and the organ started to grow again.

One instrument in France had 1400 pipes, the largest big enough for a man to crawl through. Another, built in Amiens in 1429, had 2000 pipes.

Then reaction set in. Organs had become too expensive for small churches. So a miniature organ called a 'regal' was evolved, with beating reeds like a clarinet. In 1550 a regal organ was invented so small that it could be folded up and fitted into a hollowed-out bible. It was called a bible regal, the backs of the bible being used as bellows.

Electricity was added to the organ in the 1860s, to aid the operation of the complexity of stops and to increase air pressure. The cinema organs of the 1930s were a mixture of electronic devices and windblown pipes, coupled with endless mechanical gadgets such as motor horns and drums. The Hammond and similar organs produce their tones with vibrations caused by light waves.

The largest organ ever built is in Atlantic City, U.S.A. It has seven manuals, 33,112 pipes ranging from 3/16ths of an inch to 64 feet, a range of seven octaves and the volume of 25 brass bands!

43

14 Three Early Masters

The three men who completed this task and stood at the end of the Middle Ages opening the gateway to the Renaissance, were Giovanni Palestrina, Orlandus Lassus, and William Byrd.

Born within a few years of each other, the paths of the first two ran very close as masters of the high polyphonic period of church music.

It has been said that there were no really great musicians in the Middle Ages—just a legion of gifted, talented, hard-working pioneers who were laying the foundations for the greats to come.

Organist and choirmaster at 18, choirmaster of St. Peter's, Rome, at 26, composer of the first church music to be dedicated to a Pope at 29, Palestrina had an amazing capacity for work. At first engaged in composing masses to order for an aristocratic Italian family—five in one

Giovanni Palestrina (c. 1525-1594) called The Father of Modern Music

year, seven in another – he then travelled to Rome and settled down to his life work of writing masses, madrigals, motets and music of all kinds, sacred and secular. His *Stabat Mater* for eight voices (part of the Catholic church service) is held to be one of the greatest musical glories of all time.

This remarkable man fell victim in the middle of his career to one of the plagues that swept across Europe in those days. His family and his patrons were wiped out, but somehow Palestrina managed to survive and build his life all over again, this time combining the strangely different careers of master furrier and master composer.

In 1562 the Church issued some stern new rules to composers and singers. If they wished to enjoy the patronage of the Church, they said, they must ensure:

1 That Mass was not sung too quickly
2 That popular songs were not used as a basis for masses
3 That too much counterpoint was not used to cover up the words and 'give only empty pleasure to the ear'
4 That no 'evil-thinking and impure' harmony be used.

But Palestrina took all this in his stride, continuing to turn out perfectly balanced harmony and counterpoint. In all, he composed a hundred masses and six hundred motets with such fine writing that he has come to be known as The Father of Modern Music. When he died, 15,000 people walked from his home town to Rome, singing his music.

His contemporary, Orlandus Lassus, was no less gifted or successful. It is remarkable that two such giants should have lived at the same time and worked in the same sphere. At 21, Lassus was maestro of the Lateran in Rome, at 24 he was a director of music at the Court.

Equally famous as a composer – he wrote over 2000 works – and as a trainer of choirs, Lassus' most important contribution was his mastery of the harmonic knowledge that had been so laboriously built up in the many centuries of the Middle Ages.

Lassus thought in terms of harmony – as does a modern composer. He did not, as so many of his contemporaries and predecessors did, conceive a line of melody and then add harmony to it. The total sound sprang into his mind, complete. His writing was closer to modern concepts than anyone who had gone before him.

Although he wrote much formal church music, his talent inclined more to the expression of human tenderness. Whereas Palestrina is remembered for his masses, Lassus is remembered for his motets.

These two great musicians died within a few months of each other, Lassus having for some years previously suffered from acute mental depression. His four sons were all musicians.

Contemporary with Palestrina and Lassus, and ranking with them, was William Byrd, born in 1542 in Lincoln. Like them he achieved important status very early, being organist of Lincoln Cathedral at 20 and, later, of the Chapel Royal, Westminster.

Apart from being one of the Fathers of English Music and the composer of madrigals, church music, string music and anthems of sublime quality, Byrd must also have been an able politician.

A firm Roman Catholic, he lived through the reigns of both Elizabeth and James I, wrote an outstanding Anglican Great Service for the first and equally great Masses for the second. He lived happily and successfully until he was eighty.

Orlandus Lassus (c. 1532-1594) playing one of his own works on the virginals

15 The First Operas

Scene from The Beggar's Opera, *produced in 1728*

At the end of the sixteenth century some wild young men in Florence were meeting secretly in a café to discuss a revolutionary idea. It was not to pull down the government, or start a war, or anything like that – but to them it was equally exciting.

It was that actors in plays should *sing* the words instead of speaking them.

Plays there had been; singing there had been; singing during plays there had been. But telling the story in singing? That was really new. They tried it and it was a big success.

But it took a great musician, Claudio Monteverdi, to make the idea work satisfactorily. In 1607 he wrote the first real opera (the word 'opera' merely means 'work') and called it *The Orpheus Fable*. It was a huge success, not only then but long after in the twentieth century, when it was revived.

There had, of course, been many plays with music before this – the Miracle plays of the eleventh century, masques (a mixture of poetry, dancing, acting, costume, singing and instrumental music), pastorals (music and ballet) and others. But the difference is that in opera the music is an essential part, not merely an incidental extra.

But almost as soon as the new art had been launched it ran into trouble. At first, music was subordinate to the words and story. Movement and acting were strictly limited – actors who could sing, or singers who could act, were rare. To relieve this situation the 'aria' (air or melody) began to dominate the words so that quite often phrases and sentences were mangled out of sense in order to make them fit the flowery arias. Then the singers began to ornament the arias just to show off their vocal skills and both the words and the tunes suffered.

At first, operas had consisted mostly of 'recitatives' (spoken music) in order to get the story across. But this turned out to be dull entertainment if persisted with for long stretches. So the arias took over. Then there came orchestral interludes to give the singers a chance to catch their breath and the stage hands time to change the scenery. There were even bits of comedy singing inserted between the acts – the beginning of what is called *Opera Buffa* (Opera for Clowns).

It was a long time before all this conflict was brought into some kind of balance. It was not until the composer came to be in complete charge, balancing the requirements of words and music, that opera really succeeded. Even today, however, it is regarded as a difficult art form and without some understanding of all the skills that go into it, it can all too easily become somewhat boring and occasionally ridiculous as well. It takes a considerable appreciation of musical composition and of the high arts of singing not to be put off by the sight of a dying hero, wounded in a dozen places, spending several minutes reaching for his top notes before expiring.

But there is a good deal more to opera than this. Opera has been described as the most ambitious invention of the classical age in music – recitatives and arias, solos, duets, trios, quartets and more; the intermingling of soprano, contralto, tenor, baritone and bass voices; orchestral writing that contains preludes, fugues, dance forms and symphonic writing – but blends perfectly with the vocal activity. Add stage spectacle to this, costume design and emotional acting, and it is a marvel not that the mixture contains some in consistencies but that it works at all. There is no doubt in the minds of those millions of people in all countries, who flock to the opera houses, that it does succeed, even today with all the rival attractions to lure them away to easier art forms.

Since the first operas came from Italy, it has not unreasonably always been thought of as characteristic of that country, although German, French, Russian and British composers have long since shown their mastery of this form.

The Italian composer Scarlatti who flourished at the end of the seventeenth century, wrote 115 operas and was founder of the Neapolitan School.

By the eighteenth century the shape of opera had become pretty well set and singers noted for their pure tone and brilliant techniques were becoming the new musical stars. This type of singing was called *bel canto* (beautiful song).

Another type was that developed by Italian singers called *castrati* (men with high-pitched boy's voices). These singers became immensely popular and enormously well paid. Wagner at one time was so fascinated by their pure high tones that he contemplated writing an entire opera featuring them.

Handel, although of German birth, was a great and successful writer of opera in the Italian style during the early eighteenth century and made a fortune in London with this kind of musical entertainment.

But it was in Vienna that opera was reaching its peak in the hands of gifted composers like Gluck and Mozart (*Figaro*, in Italian, 1786; and *The Magic Flute* in German, in 1791).

By the nineteenth century we reach the great composers of opera like Bellini, Donizetti, Rossini and Verdi, who is dealt with in more detail in a later chapter.

There is hardly a great name in music who has not devoted his talents to opera – Beethoven, Wagner, Berlioz, Bizet, Tchaikovsky, Massenet, St. Saens, Albeniz, Richard Strauss, Shosta-kovich – the list is endless.

In Britain the list ranges from Henry Purcell through Ethel Smyth, Holst and Vaughan Williams to Benjamin Britten.

With all this tremendous volume of talent being poured into it it is understandable how highly the art of opera is regarded. Opera and the symphony are, indeed, the twin mountain peaks of music.

But not always. Purcell's opera, *Dido and Aeneas*, was expressly written for a girls school in 1689 because they asked the distinguished composer if he would be kind enough to write something to celebrate a special occasion. No doubt they had in mind some simple hymn that could be sung by the girls and one can but guess at what the headmistress thought when the great man came up with a complete opera for large cast, chorus and full orchestra!

Sir Francis Drake was so fond of music that he took musicians with him on his long voyages

48

16 Music – the Food of Love

Queen Elizabeth I was devoted to music. She was an accomplished player on the virginal and she helped with money and patronage the fortunes and careers of musicians (as well as playwrights and poets).

The virginal was very much an instrument of the period. It was a direct descendant of the ancient psaltery (a D-shaped flat box with strings stretched across it, plucked by the fingers), made considerably bigger and equipped with a keyboard. Contemporary and often confused with it, were the harpsichord, the spinet and the clavichord. All of these were keyboard instruments with strings that were activated by the action of the piano-like keys.

The main difference was that of shape – the harpsichord was shaped like a harp laid flat on its side with the keyboard at the small side of the triangle; the spinet had the same basic pattern of a harp on its side, but with the keyboard at the long side; the virginal was almost the same as the spinet but had the strings at an angle. The early clavichord was different from all the others in that it had less strings than keys, each string being made to produce several different notes.

All these instruments had a pleasant sweet tone which made them ideal instruments for drawing-room usage.

The story goes that the virginal was named after Elizabeth, the Virgin Queen, but – alas for that romantic idea – it was known under that name before she was born. A more likely reason for the name is that it was named after an essential part of the mechanism for plucking the strings, called a rod or jack (*virga* in Latin). Or, just possibly, because it was usually played by young girls.

Other familiar instruments of the period were the viols (stringed instruments with frets, like a guitar but played with a bow) which were made up into families of different sizes kept in velvet-lined oak boxes, hence the phrase 'a chest of viols.' When used on their own they were called a 'consort;' when used with wind instruments, a 'broken consort.'

The most popular wind instruments were the recorders, made in different sizes, just like those in use today. The lute was also used, either in its more usual small size or in a larger version called a 'theorbo.' Then there were the 'cittern' and 'gittern,' two other instruments of the lute type.

Queen Elizabeth, besides playing and singing, liked to have musical instruments very much in evidence at her royal functions, both public and private. She also helped the purely commercial side of music by granting to William Byrd and his older composer-friend and teacher Thomas Tallis a twenty-one year monoply to print music and music paper. But neither was much of a business man and the monoply was sold to Thomas East, one of the first of the successful music publishers. East poured out printed music in a tremendous spate, and Byrd was one of the first to benefit, turning out psalms and religious motets along with what today would be described as pop songs, such as his *The Carman's Whistle*.

But the crowning achievement musically was the madrigal. Having originated in Italy, they were non-religious songs arranged for several voices and making much use of counterpoint or 'part singing' sometimes including parts for viols. Madrigal singing dominated the Elizabethan scene for forty years, and the golden age of the Madrigal lasted from the time of the Spanish Armada (1588) until Cromwell first entered Parliament (1628).

Madrigal singing was the popular family entertainment in which all joined – masters, mistresses, children and servants. 'Come round for an evening of madrigals' must have been a familiar invitation. One of the books of madrigals published at the time by East has the description 'For Gentleman and Merchants to Sing.

A somewhat lighter form of the madrigal was the 'ballett,' characterised by a 'fa-la-la' chorus to which the singers used to dance.

Sir Francis Drake loved music so much that he found room in his tiny ships for musicians so that during his voyages he could dine and be entertained by the music of viols.

17 Bach—the Greatest of Them All

In the opinion of many people the greatest musician who ever lived was Johann Sebastian Bach. Born in 1685, he was one of a very large family of musicians – some 53 of them occupied positions as organists, teachers and so on.

The earliest trace of musical gifts in the family seem to have been with Johann's great-great-grandfather; a miller who loved to play the zither, a kind of closed wooden box with 30 or 40 strings stretched over it.

Whether it was the zither or some other unknown factor in the family make up, it is a fact that from then on the Bach family produced an unparalled run of gifted musicians. In fact, there were so many of them who became noteworthy that one has to take the unusual step of using all their names (instead of just Beethoven or Handel or Mozart) to identify them. There were Carl Philipp Emanuel Bach, Johann Christoph Bach, Johann Christian Bach, Johann Christoph Friedrich Bach and so on and so on. But Johann Sebastian is the one we are concerned with and he was the greatest of them all.

His parents died when he was quite young and he was brought up by an elder brother, who was also a musician. From the very earliest age, Johann Sebastian had been taught music. Indeed, in that family, how could it have been otherwise? He could play the violin, the organ and the other keyboard instruments almost as soon as he could walk.

One of the many stories told about the young Johann Sebastian is about a book of musical pieces, a rare and valuable thing in those days, which his elder brother kept under lock and key. Young Johann wanted to borrow it, but his brother refused to lend it. Perhaps he thought of him as just a tiresome young child not fit to be trusted with valuable objects. After all, how many of us would recognise a genius in our family, especially in the person of a young schoolboy?

But the cupboard had a glass front with one of the panes loose. Young J. S. used to steal down in the middle of the night, work the loose pane out, get hold of the book and sit up half the night copying it. But big brother found out and was so enraged that he destroyed the copy J. S. had so laboriously made. But it didn't matter because the boy had memorised all the pieces as he had been copying them!

As he grew up Johann Sebastian held various musical jobs. Choirboy, violinist in the orchestra of a local prince, organist of the town church, chief musician in a provincial court and as principal of music of all its associated churches.

Although this sounds like an unhindered series of successes, life was not as easy as that. Firstly, J. S. found that he was not very good at teaching and controlling choir boys. He lacked disciplined control and easily became impatient when the boys seemed to him to be stupid about their music. So he did the sensible thing, he concentrated on something he liked better, the organ.

He became a brilliant performer and writer of music for this instrument. As a player he was said to be the best of his day. When he heard that a well-known organist was to visit a nearby town, he would walk many miles there and back – he had no money for coach fares – just to listen, and if possible, talk to the visiting celebrity. It was during this part of his life that he wrote many of his most famous organ pieces.

He felt the need to travel in order to study and widen his knowledge. He visited various centres of music, always keeping himself by playing. He became an expert in Italian instrumental music, German organ preludes, and French harpsichord music, as well as in chorales, motets, cantatas and string trios.

In those days Germany was a collection of small principalities, each ruled over by a local prince. Each court maintained its own orchestra, choir and musicians. With all his knowledge, Johann Sebastian was ideally suited to become chief musician at some such wealthy court. He chose to take a job as second in command at the Saxon court at Weimar, but when his chief died he was not promoted to his post. So, he moved to another court at Cothen and stayed there for five years. During this time he composed some of his greatest music – violin concertos, cello

Johann Sebastian Bach at the organ

51

An 18th century musical instrument workshop, from Diderot's Encyclopedia

sonatas, the first book of his magnificent *Forty-Eight Preludes and Fugues for Keyboard*, and the illustrious *Brandenburg Concertos*, of which there were six for various orchestral combinations. They got their name from the fact that they were commissioned by the Margrave (prince) of Brandenburg.

Then a new job loomed, Cantor of the famed choir school of Leipzig, St. Thomas's. He was asked to write a test piece as a kind of audition – the *St. John Passion*. A Passion is a musical work of religious significance telling of the last days in the life of Christ, usually calling for a large choir, orchestra, organ and soloists. Bach completed the test piece in ten weeks and, as time has shown, it was a masterpiece. But the city fathers of Leipzig gave him the job only after two other musicians had turned it down!

Whilst at Leipzig he wrote four other Passions, including the most famous, the *Saint Matthew Passion*, the *B Minor Mass* and the second volume of the *Forty-Eight Preludes and Fugues*.

His twenty-five years' stay in St. Thomas' School began badly. He wanted to re-organise everything but the city fathers wanted things left as they were. Although he succeeded pretty well, the work wore him down. Apart from his writing and teaching, he directed nearly 1,500 cantata performances in the first ten years.

He was twice married and had twenty children, of whom several became famous musicians. He died in 1750, aged 65, having lost his sight several years previously.

One of the great problems of the day came about through the gradual predominance of instrumental music over sung music. There is a very slight difference between pairs of notes such as B sharp and C, or C sharp and D flat, which singers could allow for but which instruments such as the organ could not. So compromises had to be worked out, allowing the pairs of notes to be sounded by one key. This is called 'temperament' and Bach's famous *Forty-Eight Preludes and Fugues* were written in every key to show how a 'well-tempered keyboard' could move from key to key without difficulty. Designed more or less as demonstrations, they were, through Bach's genius, all masterpieces.

52

18 Handel – a Man of Society

There must have been something special about the year 1685, for it produced not only Johann Sebastian Bach but George Frederic Handel. However, whereas Bach was born into an atmosphere of music and encouraged almost from birth to become a musician, Handel met with every obstacle in following the profession of which he was to become one of the great geniuses.

His father was a barber-surgeon in the Court of the Duke of Saxony – a curious combination of jobs which was normal at that time. Barbers were limited to trimming beards, tending wigs, blood-letting and drawing teeth, whereas surgeons were allowed to do larger jobs but were prohibited from 'barbery and shaving'. It wasn't until about 1745 that they became separate occupations.

Perhaps it was because Handel Senior knew so much about court life from the inside that he was horrified when his son began to show signs of musical talent – musicians had very little status in those days, and received very little pay. He strictly forbade his son to have anything to do with music.

A more understanding relative smuggled a clavichord, a boxlike forerunner of the piano, into the attic so that the boy could teach himself to play. So entranced was young George with this wonderful toy that he used to lie awake at night until he was sure his parents were asleep, then creep up into the attic and play very very softly to himself in the dead of night.

But not quite softly enough. After a while he became a little more enthusiastic and played a little louder. His parents woke up, soon tracked down the midnight sounds of music and George received a beating and a warning never to misbehave himself again. He was, of course, heart-broken, for without music life did not seem worth living. However, his father was adamant.

It was not until an important person at the Duke's Court heard this story and urged Father Handel to let the boy have his way that he finally gave in, although insisting that George learned something else as well.

Thus encouraged, George took off like a rocket. By the age of eleven he was learning organ, harpsichord, violin, oboe, harmony and counterpoint. By the time he was eighteen he was exceedingly skilful in all these subjects – and had passed his law exams as well. In addition, he learned to speak fluent French, Italian and English; the Italian so that he could talk to Italian musicians!

With all this talent and training behind him, it was a bit of a let down that the first job he got was as a violinist in the opera house at Hamburg, a start which seemed to justify his father's gloomiest forebodings, for orchestral musicians in those days earned only a few shillings a week.

With Handel the genius-talent was too strong for things to stay that way for long. Within two years he had had his first opera produced and had received an invitation to go to Florence to join the retinue of the mighty Medici household. He jumped at the chance to travel abroad, unlike Bach, who never left his own country.

He was a great success there and played and composed in the principal cities of Italy for four years. The Italians were amazed at his skill, which was saying something, because Italy was the home of music and musicians. Then he had an offer to return to Hanover and join the Court of the Elector (a kind of prince) as chief of music, or *kapellmeister*. He was a great success but his desire for travel was still strong and he left to try his fortune in London.

This was to be the peak of his success and where he spent the rest of his life. In London he wrote an opera, *Rinaldo*, which was such an overnight sensation that he became the darling of the English Court. So much so, in fact, that his old master, the Elector of Hanover, became jealous and ordered him back to Germany. Reluctantly, Handel returned, but not for long. The little Court of Hanover seemed small and dull compared with being the toast of London so, defying his master's orders Handel returned to London and continued in his great success there. By an amazing twist of fate, the Elector ot Hanover became King George I of England. When he arrived in London he refused to have anything to do with Handel, whose success was suddenly dimmed as a result.

It took Handel some time to get back into favour, which he did with adroit flattery. The King used to enjoy having parties on the river, with boatloads of richly-dressed courtiers surrounding the royal barge. The story goes that Handel contrived to hide himself and some musicians on another barge and play some music he had specially composed for the occasion. The King was delighted with the music and asked who had composed it. When he found out that it was Handel he sent for him and forgave him. The music was the now famous *Water Music*.

Handel went on to ever greater fame, writing some of the finest oratorios ever conceived. (An oratorio is like an opera on a religious subject except that it uses no scenery or costumes and the singers do not act. It is called an oratorio because this style of music was first performed in the oratory, or small chapel, of a big church). The most famous of these was the *Messiah*, and it is said that when King George II (the son of

Handel's first patron) heard the great *Hallelujah Chorus* he was so excited that he stood up. All the audience followed suit, it being court etiquette that no one should sit while the King stood. That was in 1745 and to this very day the audience often stands when the *Hallelujah Chorus* is played although few of them know why.

As Handel climbed higher and higher he inevitably got mixed up in politics and incurred enemies. One of his rivals wrote an opera in parody of Handel's Italianate style, making fun of the mixture of music, politics and court intrigue which Handel practised. This was *The Beggar's Opera* and is still performed today. Handel went on involving himself in ever more costly operatic adventures, not all of them financially successful. Eight years before he died, at the age of 74, he went blind and had to rely on his copyist to get his music down on paper.

He was buried in Westminster Abbey, a great man of his adopted country. Beethoven said of him: 'Learn from him how to create great effects with simple means.'

The first performance of Handel's Water Music *took place on the Thames in 1715*

The young Mozart at the harpsichord

19 Mozart – the Four-year-old Genius

The word genius is all too often used without justification, signifying as it does a capacity so far ahead of everyone else that it stands alone.

Whether it is a good thing to be a genius, and whether it brings happiness to be so much better than anyone else, is another question.

That Mozart was a genius nobody disputes; it is also true that he died at the age of thirty-five – ill, unhappy and so poor that he was buried in a pauper's grave.

His father, Leopold Mozart, was a better-than-average violinist and composer at the court of the Prince Archbishop of Salzburg. He wrote many symphonies and other works, published a book on violin playing and produced two very gifted children.

The Mozarts had seven children, of which only two survived – but what a remarkable two they were!

Maria Anna was born in 1751 and at an early age her father started to teach her the harpsichord. She very rapidly showed signs of outstanding talent and father Leopold, recognising that he had a prodigy on his hands, drove her even harder.

Five years after Anna Maria (whose pet name in the family was Nannerl) was born, a son arrived in the Mozart household – Wolfgang Amadeus. He, too, had a nickname – Wolferl. He also had something else – a talent so remarkable as to be almost unbelievable.

It was first noticed at the age of three, when Wolfgang went into the room where Anna Maria was having her several-hours-long lesson on the clavier (short name for any home keyboard intrument of the time), listened until the lesson was over, then said 'I can play Nannerl's piece' – and did, his tiny fingers barely able to depress the keys.

Father Leopold realised that he had another prodigy on his hands and immediately started the child on music lessons. By the age of four he was good enough to play in public. By the age of five he began to compose. His first effort was a minuet.

By the age of six he made his debut as a concert performer as a brilliant harpsichordist, and began a series of tours as a child prodigy,

A famous painting by Carmontelle – Mozart with His Father and Sister

visiting the courts of Europe with his father and sister.

These tours were a fantastic success. At the age of eight he was invited to dine with the King of France. Then in 1764, he went to London to play for King George III.

By his ninth birthday he was not only an international celebrity, but a master of several languages in which he was able to discourse learnedly with the great musicians of the period on such subjects as the poetic keyboard compositions of France, the vivacity of Italian opera, and the sonata form with J. C. Bach, whom he met in London.

While in London, father Leopold arranged daily concerts from twelve to three, to which Londoners of both high and low degree flocked just to stare at the wonder child, paying half-a-crown a head, equivalent to two or three pounds today.

With Munich, Linz, Vienna and London conquered, Paris and Amsterdam soon followed – an ever-widening circle of non-stop concerts, interviews, meetings, talks, that lasted for four years.

A great deal has been written about how father Leopold drove his two gifted children like slaves, never letting them behave like ordinary children (which, of course, they were not) and permitting nothing but work, work, work and still more work – appearances, endless practice, travelling over long distances by coach, seldom sleeping more than a few nights in the same bed.

But father Leopold knew only too well how hard it was to make a living as a composer and player in those days, how without princely patronage and a job at court it was a question of scraping a few pennies by giving lessons to the children of the wealthy. He knew, too, that very seldom did child prodigies fulfill their bright promise – by their teens they were usually mediocrities. Perhaps he thought that he would make money for his children while they were still prodigies. Whatever his reasons, he drove them unmercifully – but none of the family finished up rich, as we shall see.

The family returned to Salzburg, where Wolfgang took up an appointment as court musician. But he still gave concerts and in 1769, when Wolfgang was thirteen, the kindly old Prince Archbishop let them off for another two years to tour Italy. This was the boy's first visit to Rome and he was particularly looking forward to hearing some music in the Pope's private chapel – especially a celebrated *Miserere*, the setting of one of the Psalms used in the Roman Catholic service. Although many had heard this famous piece, nobody was allowed to see, much less take away, the music itself.

Wolfgang and his father went to the service, heard the long and complicated piece and returned to their lodging to discuss it. After his father had gone to bed, the thirteen-old-boy sat up all night and wrote out the work from memory – after only one hearing! Father Leopold, well accustomed as he was to his son's genius, could scarcely believe it. It was not until he had been again to the service, with the manuscript in his hand, that the elder Mozart was

Wolfgang Amadeus Mozart (1770-1827)

compelled to admit that his son had, indeed, accomplished this fantastic feat.

The Pope got to hear about it and sent for them. Expecting trouble, they were relieved, to say the least, when the Pope asked the boy to play for him and rewarded him with the Order of the Golden Spur.

But father Leopold knew that Wolfgang could not go on being a child prodigy for ever and that the time had come for him to develop musically into a composer and conductor. So back to Salzburg they went, Mozart to concentrate on composing.

An opera of his was accepted by Milan opera house and once again the indulgent Prince Archbishop gave him time off to travel to Italy. The visit was a success but when he returned to Salzburg bad news awaited him. The kindly old Archbishop had died and had been replaced by another man, who had little enthusiasm for having an internationally-famous personage on his staff. He believed that musicians, who

Correction

Caption should read:

Wolfgang Amadeus Mozart (1756-1791)

ranked with servants, should be kept in their place – which was one rank below the cooks. Sometimes they were compelled to wear livery, like the coachmen.

This did not suit Mozart at all. Accustomed to be feted in the Courts of Europe and treated with adulation, the Archbishop's determination to puncture Mozart's self-esteem soon led to battles which Mozart was bound to lose.

Now began bad times for the family. Mozart was not allowed to travel but was stuck in the dull little town of Salzburg, doing routine jobs in the church. Also, the Archbishop began to bear down on Mozart's father, who began to fear for his job.

Then came a commission – to write a comic opera for the Elector of Bavaria for the carnival in Munich. Mozart jumped at the chance and the opera brought back a touch of the old adulation. Mozart was once again the hero of the hour and returned to Salzburg in triumph.

But this only worsened the relationship between the Archbishop and Mozart. When the Archbishop travelled to Vienna he took Mozart with him, partly no doubt to keep an eye on him. Mozart was invited to play before the Emperor, who was also in Vienna at the time. But the Archbishop flatly refused to allow him the time off, even for that.

This was the last straw. Mozart threatened the Archbishop that if he were not allowed time off he would resign. This was just the opportunity the Archbishop was waiting for – this was rank insubordination, and from an inferior servant at that!

Mozart was summarily dismissed – some stories say he was actually thrown out of the Archbishop's palace by force.

Mozart realised that he had at last got his freedom and started to try to earn his living as a freelance composer. He was now twenty-five and ready to conquer the musical world of Vienna. But Vienna proved itself coldly indifferent. The boy wonder was forgotten and the young composer was unknown.

It was Haydn whom Mozart had met when he had visited Vienna eight years previously, and who had enormously influenced Mozart's Salzburg composing, who took the young man under his wing. Haydn was twenty-five years older but he recognised the genius of the younger man's writing and did his utmost to bring it to the attention of Viennese critics, impressarios and publishers.

But it was still a very rough time for Mozart. He was earning a meagre living as a concert performer – but the glittering boyhood days were gone, there were many virtuosi in Vienna with established reputations and greater popularity. His music was considered too 'way out' to attract publishers – and, in any case, publication in those days brought only a small outright payment and no further income, there being no copyright law.

Mozart by now was married – but disastrously. His wife was a spendthrift and disposed of Mozart's meagre earnings as soon as they came in. Haydn's marriage was also a failure and the two men found sympathy in each other's plight. Haydn had no children and was always adopting them; the Mozarts had a new-born son.

But if Mozart's private life and finances were a failure his music was not. Great works poured from his pen – works of pure genius, like *Figaro*, *Don Giovanni*, *The Magic Flute*, forty-one symphonies – including the superb 'Jupiter', chamber music, piano works, vocal music.

Haydn, who had so much influenced Mozart in the beginning, eventually recognised a talent even greater than his own and his later works show the unmistakable influence of the younger man.

Mozart drove himself with even more fury. His three greatest symphonies – the E flat, the G minor and the 'Jupiter' – were all written in six weeks in 1788.

But these supreme masterpieces brought in relatively little money and Mozart was forced back into touring as a concert virtuoso. Wherever he played he had his compositions on sale – over a score of concertos and sonatas have survived, and he was always ready to write music for the latest dances, or showpieces for other virtuosi, such as the Clarinet Quintet.

But although this provided a living it did no more. He died in Vienna in 1791, aged thirty-five, having produced music which has seldom been approached for sheer beauty and magnificence and never surpassed.

20 Beethoven – the Deaf Composer

One of the unexpected results of the hugely successful European tours of the Mozart children was to arouse the envy of a musician employed by a minor German prince.

This man was a singer, not a very good one, a drunkard, and poor. When a son was born to him he determined that he would make him as successful as the young Mozart, who was fourteen when the baby Ludwig was born into the van Beethoven family in 1770. (The 'van', by the way, did not indicate aristocratic birth like the German 'von' – but merely that the family was of Flemish extraction).

Almost as soon as the boy could walk he entered into a rigorous course of musical instruction, his father standing over him for hours as he practised the piano (which by now was beginning to replace the harpsichord) and violin.

Although he became a good performer and was able to give recitals as a boy in his teens, and to deputise for the court organist by the time he was eleven, it was not as a player that he was to make his name but as a composer. He published his first work when he was thirteen and if his father had had any musical perception he might have recognised the first signs of the genius that his son was to display in later years. But he did not – all he was interested in was that the boy should make money playing the piano, so he

The deaf Beethoven being lionised by Viennese society, which he mostly treated with contempt

gave it out that the composition was the work of a child of ten.

But although his first attempt at composing went unremarked, young Ludwig got the job of deputy organist at the court when he was thirteen, and also played the viola in the court theatre.

Still he kept composing. At seventeen he visited Vienna and played before Mozart, then thirty-one and long past his child prodigy days. Mozart was considerably impressed and said 'That young man will make a great noise in the world some day' – a generous tribute as well as being a very accurate forecast.

But although Beethoven was to become recognised as the greatest symphonic writer of all time, he was comparatively slow to develop, partly perhaps because of his upbringing, but partly through the absence of sound training in composition.

He was aware of this latter defect and tried his utmost to correct it. He had some instruction from Mozart, and some from Haydn when that old master returned to Vienna from London. Vienna was the centre of modern music and Beethoven determined to settle there. With the aid of his princely employer he was enabled to make various visits to the city and by the time he was twenty-one he decided to give up his job as a court musician – a very risky thing to do in those days – and make his living as a composer and teacher.

Haydn was very kind to him, charged him a ridiculously small fee for tuition – which was not very helpful, as a matter of fact, because Beethoven was already reaching out to horizons beyond Haydn's grasp – and introduced him into Viennese musical society.

The Viennese aristocracy took the young man to their hearts. This was remarkable, because Beethoven was arrogant, rude, openly contemptuous of their aristocratic birth, and was given to bursts of blazing bad temper – even to those who were supporting him.

Yet they not only tolerated him but sent their sons and daughters to him for lessons in music. He had, despite his boorishness, a great charm of manner, enormous vitality, an impressive appearance and total self-confidence. He was, in fact, a 'personality' as well as being a

man of genius, and these two attributes were seemingly enough to overcome all his other defects. Whereas Mozart, in the same city at the same period, and certainly as much a genius in his own way, failed to do more than scrape out a living, Beethoven, fourteen years his junior, roared through Viennese society like a raging lion, hypnotising everyone with whom he came into contact.

In 1795, when he was twenty-five, he published his piano trios and this nearly caused a breach between him and Haydn.

Although he had written and published many works before these, Beethoven regarded them as the beginning of his mature life as a composer and described them as Opus 1 (opus is the Latin word for 'work' and composers of this period were in the habit of numbering their works as they completed them – Op. 1, Op. 2 and so on).

He took them to 63-year-old Haydn for comment, the older man being not only his teacher but his friend and sponsor into Viennese society as well. One of the trios was 'way out' and Haydn advised the young man not to publish it. But Beethoven flew into a rage and refused to take any notice. It is a tribute to the underlying charm of Beethoven's personality that this row did nothing to disturb the affectionate father-son relationship of the two men.

By this time Beethoven was living rent-free in the house of Prince Lichnowsky, one of his many aristocratic admirers. His reputation as a pianist was more than sufficient to ensure him a good income and he was the first composer to make a good living from the publication of his works.

And yet he lived in complete squalor and disorder. His irascible nature caused him to fight with all the impresarios, patrons and publishers – his money affairs were in complete chaos, for he would neither manage them himself nor allow anyone else to manage them for him.

At the time of his greatest success he was being pursued for debt and living in a welter of shabby clothes, insufficient meals and domestic upheaval. He moved from lodging to lodging, partly because landladies would not put up with him, but equally because he would not put

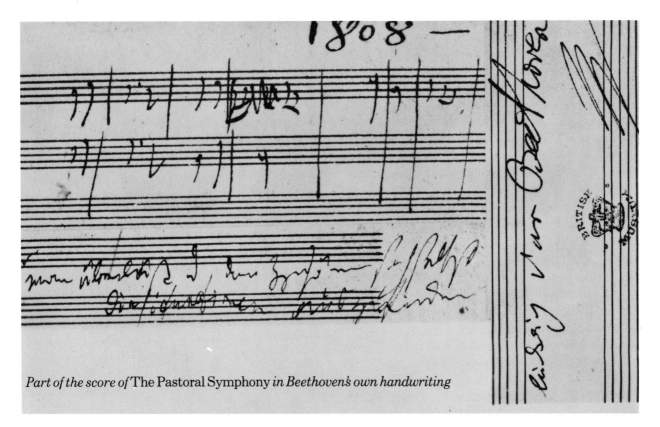

Part of the score of The Pastoral Symphony *in Beethoven's own handwriting*

up with them. On one occasion, the story goes, when something he was writing would not come out right, he threw a jug of water at the ceiling and banged the furniture about.

At this time Napoleon was conquering Europe and Beethoven saw in him the spirit of revolution that he himself so worshipped. Napoleon was his hero and his third symphony was entitled *Bonaparte* and dedicated to him. Then he learned that Napoleon had accepted the crown and title of Emperor and was outraged. He tore off the title page, erased the dedication, and called the work the *Eroica* (the Heroic).

This work expressed not the story of Napoleon, but Beethoven's attitude to life. He was a born rebel in social matters as well as music. It was, for instance, the convention of the time to wear neatly powdered wigs, carefully coiffured by court barbers. Beethoven flatly refused to have anything to do with such artificiality. He not only wore no wig but let his own hair go unpowdered and looking as if he had just got up. Mozart had set out to challenge society and had been defeated by it; Beethoven took it by the scruff of the neck and kicked it

around, and still kept his friends, despite his rough treatment of them. On one occasion he stormed angrily out of Prince Lichnowsky's house when his long-suffering host asked him to play to some of Napoleon's officers.

But trouble was on its way, trouble of a kind to which there was no answer. He began to go deaf. Of all the catastrophes that could possibly befall a composer, surely none could be greater than to lose his hearing.

For several years, Beethoven had been fearing the worst. By the time he was thirty he knew that doctors could do nothing for him.

He tried to conceal it. He could play in public without anyone noticing anything except that he tended to play very loudly. But in conversation his deafness was painfully obvious. His popularity fell away immediately.

He fled to a little village where he isolated himself from everyone, refusing to see even his closest friends, writing terrible letters full of despair. For a long time he contemplated suicide as the only possible solution to his problem.

What prevented him was either indomitable courage or extreme vanity, whichever you like. For he came to the conclusion that he was such a supreme genius that he had no right to deprive the world of the masterpieces he felt were in him.

With anyone else this would have been laughably conceited. With Beethoven it was true.

He returned to his composing and, although his manner and manners became even more impossible, his musical genius soared to still greater heights.

He did not need to hear the orchestras playing his music; he heard every note of it in his mind. The playing of the music was merely, to him, a way of letting the public know what was in his mind.

He wrote nine of the greatest symphonies the world has ever known, seventeen superb string quartets, thirty-two piano sonatas, a wonderful opera (*Fidelio*) and a stunning *Mass in D*, one of the noblest works ever to come from the pen of man. And most of this great monument of music he never heard, except in his mind.

At the first performance of his Ninth Symphony (the 'Choral') the applause at the end was tremendous, but Beethoven was totally unaware of it until a member of the orchestra seized him by the arm and turned him towards the audience so that he could *see* their reaction.

When Beethoven's younger brother died he left a son. Beethoven, who had never married, went to law to get control of the boy, then lavished such possessive love and attention on him, demanding so much, that life was impossible for both of them. Beethoven's attempts to mould the boy in the way he thought he should go – a tragic echo of his own childhood – exhausted him and even took him away from composing. For the first time he tried to conserve money, so that the boy would be properly provided for.

But it was all too much for young Karl. He failed in his exams, ran up debts he was too terrified to admit, and finally tried to commit suicide when he was just twenty-one. In his desperate rush to the injured young man, Beethoven disregarded his own comfort to such an extent that he contracted pneumonia.

He died in 1827 at the age of 56, surrounded by plans for numerous compositions.

Apart from the great works, Beethoven accomplished something else. He moved music from the courts of the princes and aristocracy to the concert halls of the people. His work demanded larger orchestras, larger halls and therefore larger audiences. He was the first great composer to reach out to a mass public.

Ludwig van Beethoven (1770-1827)

The Scottish Hebrides islands were the inspiration for Mendelssohn's Fingal's Cave *overture*

21 The Early Romantics

The short span of time between 1809 and 1811 was to see the birth of four musicians of genius.

Jacob Ludwig Felix Mendelssohn-Bartholdy was born with every advantage. Unlike so many of the musicians in this book, he was born into a wealthy and cultivated family, the son of a prosperous Hamburg banker, and the grandson of a famous philosopher, Moses Mendelssohn.

His home in Berlin was luxurious and frequented by many famous visitors – the philosopher Hegel, the sculptor Schadow, Heine, Spohr, Moscheles, Paganini and other musical celebrities. He had drawing and riding masters and two brilliant parents determined to bring up their boy with every advantage. His father even hired an orchestra every Sunday morning for the boy to practise his conducting.

He had two sisters and a younger brother and all of them rose at 5 a.m. every morning except Sunday, to commence their lessons. Abraham Mendelssohn, the father, was a deeply religious man, although he abandoned the Jewish faith and became an Evangelist, changing his name to Mendelssohn-Bartholdy. He laid down stern rules of conduct and behaviour for his children. Felix was required to compose on a regular basis, whether he felt like it or not. As a result, he turned out a good deal of inferior music as well as, in later years, some of remarkable quality.

He was an obedient boy. When his father told him to start writing light music he did so; when his father advised him to drop that and move on to more serious stuff he did that too – with equal success.

A more than brilliant pianist and outstanding composer, his life seemed just too perfect. When his father said 'Travel', he did so, travelling all over Europe, including the Scottish Hebrides, where he saw the famous Fingal's Cave that so impressed him that there and then he sketched out the overture which was to become one of his most-played works.

He married happily and had happy children. He was a success everywhere he went. At sixteen he had written a brilliantly mature octet for strings, by seventeen he had composed the beautiful overture to *A Midsummer Night's Dream*. Town director of music at Dusseldorf at twenty-four, composer of four symphonies (the first when he was fifteen) chamber music, songs, oratorios, organ sonatas, he wore himself out with overwork. He never refused anybody anything. He conducted all over Europe, including England, where he was a great favourite of Queen Victoria, who sang his music. He played the piano like a virtuoso, gave organ recitals, founded and directed a school of music and organised the erection of a monument to Bach.

Then his beloved father died and Felix was crushed. He seemed incapable of coping with this huge gap in his life, despite his manifold professional activities. His health began to fail and he plunged into a depression that was lifted only when he married happily. But his thoughts always turned back to his childhood and he wanted to re-establish the home in Berlin with

Felix Mendelssohn (1809-1847)

his brother and sisters. Then his sister Fanny died and Mendelssohn seemed inconsolable. Six months later he himself died, at the age of thirty-eight.

One of the people whom Mendelssohn met was the Polish-French Frédéric Chopin, one year older than himself and already the rage of Paris when they met in 1834. Mendelssohn was much the more mature of the two – Chopin said Mendelssohn made him feel like a trivial Parisian dandy, to which Mendelssohn replied that Chopin made him feel like a school-master – he was then twenty-five.

Like Mendelssohn, Chopin had had a happy childhood, although by no means so luxurious. Also like Mendelssohn, he was deeply attached to his father and shattered by his death.

He was a child piano prodigy with amazing powers of improvisation. Even as a youth he was a huge success in his native Warsaw, and later in Vienna. He was urged to travel but could not bring himself to leave his current girl friend, a soprano at the Warsaw Opera House. Eventually circumstances settled the matter for him when revolt against Russia broke out in Warsaw, which was then a Russian province, while he was on a visit to Vienna. There was no point in going back so he went to Paris instead where his triumph was immediate.

He was taken up by the millionaire banking family of the Rothschilds and earned large sums of money playing in the salons of the wealthy. On a concert visit to Germany he fell in love with a Polish girl he had known since childhood. They were going to get married but Chopin began to show signs of serious ill health and the girl's parents withdrew their consent.

A year later he met the famous woman novelist who went under the name of George Sand. She was seven years older than he but gave him the affectionate care he needed. This lasted for eleven years but finally broke up because of Chopin's conflicts with George Sand's son and daughter.

During this time, however, he had been pouring out masterpieces for the piano, and giving occasional recitals. In 1841 he gave a concert in Paris, about which Liszt wrote 'The hint of a wild and fiery nature, which is part of his inheritance, finds expression in strange harmonies and deliberate discords, while all his delicacy and grace is shown in a thousand

Frédéric Chopin (1810-1849)

Robert Schumann (1810-1856)

Franz Liszt (1811-1886)

touches, the thousand tiny details of an incomparable fantasy'.

After his break with George Sand, he found a new companion, Jean Stirling, a Scottish pupil of his, who urged him to visit her in Scotland. He did so, giving concerts in London, Manchester and Glasgow. In November of 1848 he gave a recital at a charity ball for Polish refugees in London. It was his last public appearance.

A year later, confined to his room in Paris, ill and suffering but still writing and sustained by his friends, he died, aged thirty-nine.

Mendelssohn and Chopin were two of a trio of mid-nineteenth-century composers called The Three Great Romantics. The third was Robert Schumann, exactly the same age as Chopin.

But unlike the others, Robert Schumann was not from a musical family. Born in Saxony, the son of a bookseller-novelist, his early life was comfortable enough and his father paid for piano lessons although he would have preferred young Robert to follow him into literary work. By the age of ten he was composing at the piano, by eleven he was giving school concerts, by fifteen his local music teacher declared that the boy had outstripped him. A year later his father died and his mother begged him to take up something reliable.

Easy-going Robert agreed, enrolled in Leipzig University to study law and plodded unsuccessfully through his courses, taking piano lessons

on the side from Leipzig's leading piano teacher, who eventually intervened and wrote to Schumann's mother undertaking to make Robert 'one of the greatest pianists now living'. Somewhat apprehensively, his mother agreed.

Impatient to make up for lost time, Schumann invented a device which clamped his little finger while he practised with the others. This ruined him for life as a pianist. But it at least allowed him to concentrate on learning harmony and counterpoint and to give full rein to his composing ability. Strangely enough, at this moment, the literary influence of his father came back to him and he started a very successful musical magazine which he was to run for ten years and from which he was to make a very comfortable living.

He married the daughter of his music teacher and rather saw himself as a successor to Beethoven, writing massive orchestral works as well as brilliant piano compositions and string quartets. He became director of the Dusseldorf orchestra, taught piano and composition at Leipzig Conservatory and conducted a men's choral society in Dresden. But although he was happy, all this work was too much. He had one nervous breakdown after another, until he reached such a desperate state that he threw himself into the Rhine. He was rescued, but only to spend the last two years of his life in a mental asylum. He died there in 1856 at the age of forty-six.

Another contemporary of The Three Great Romantics' was Hungarian-born Franz Liszt – perhaps the greatest of all virtuoso pianists. So brilliant was his technique that when Beethoven heard him he was so admiring that he flung his arms round him and kissed him. Even the irascible Wagner held him in such esteem that he trusted him with the first production of his *Lohengrin*. He wrote 400 original compositions for piano and 900 transcriptions for piano of other people's works.

After earning what was in those days the unthinkably huge sum of £60,000 a year he suddenly gave it all up, took holy orders, became known as the Abbé Liszt and lived on a few pounds a year. Unlike the others, he lived to a ripe and comfortable old age, dying in 1886 aged 75.

Niccoló Paganini was said to have sold his soul
to the devil in exchange for his marvellous skill

22 Paganini – the Devil's Disciple

This was the era of the virtuoso musician. So far, those mentioned have been those of the keyboard – piano, organ, harpsichord.

But one other player stands out among the other instrumentalists. Niccolò Paganini was, according to writers of the time, the greatest violinist who ever lived. Whether this would still be true against modern masters like Menuhin, Oistrakh or Stern it is impossible to say, there being no recorded music from that period on which to base the comparison.

Certainly the violin compositions Paganini left behind are of extreme technical difficulty. But they have all been played by twentieth-century violinists. We do not know, of course, at what speed he played them, or anything he may have added in the performance. But the probability is that it was his extraordinary personality added to his technical mastery that made him the legend that he is.

Born of poor parents in Genoa in 1782, by the turn of the century the boy had devoted such intensive study to the violin that he was far ahead of all other performers of the day. Added to this inhuman perseverance and tireless practice, Paganini was gifted with abnormally strong and sinewy fingers that were likened to 'steel snakes', plus a bowing arm of such muscular strength and control that it 'sawed through technical difficulties like a sabre'.

The hours, days, months, years of Paganini's early life were filled with unremitting practice, practice, and then more practice. Any less iron-strong determination would have collapsed under the strain that he imposed on himself.

Soon he had mastered every piece of violin music in existence and began writing his own. *La Campanella* is perhaps the most famous, but there were many other works for solo and unaccompanied violin.

Even the great masters of other instruments, such as Liszt, himself the most dazzlingly brilliant pianist of his day, were astounded at Paganini's execution and wrote works for him of stunning technical difficulty, as if to challenge his mastery. Paganini polished them all off with ease.

The stories about him are countless. One is that having played some immensely difficult piece he would then cut three of the four strings and announce that he would play the work equally well with one string. Another was that he would discard his bow and play a concerto with a walking stick.

He invented new techniques when all the known hazards had been mastered – like *treble-stopping* (playing on three strings at once), and a wider range of harmonics (an extra series of notes produced by touching the strings very lightly instead of pressing them down firmly) than any other player had even thought possible.

But the best story of all is that he was not human – based on the belief that no ordinary mortal could play as he did. Or, failing that, that he was in league with the devil, who helped him along. Indeed, one Viennese writer swore that he saw 'The Evil One' materialise alongside Paganini on the concert platform and guide his flying fingers!

He travelled triumphantly throughout Europe, reaching Britain in 1831 and amassing profits from that single visit of over £16,000 – or something like £200,000 in modern currency. The poor Genoese boy had become wealthy and famous indeed.

At the height of all this he suddenly announced that he was giving up the violin and taking up a *really* difficult instrument – the guitar. There is no record of how he did with that instrument but he left a number of very difficult pieces for it, so presumably his uncanny mastery extended to that instrument as well.

Because he had acquired a new Stradivarius viola, he commissioned Berlioz to write a solo viola part in the former's symphony *Harold In Italy* (the Harold being the character in Byron's poem *Childe Harold*), but he never got round to playing it – perhaps because the viola was not playing *all* the time!

Antonio Stradivari on one of his long walks looking for the perfect wood for his violins

23 Stradivarius – the Violin Maker

Paganini, like many great violinists before and after him, played and treasured violins made by Antonio Stradivari (or Stradivarius, the Latinised form of his name).

He lived in the early seventeenth century in a mountain village in Northern Italy, Cremona, which had become a centre for the manufacture of violins. He had been a pupil of Nicola Amati, also famous as a maker of much-prized violins. The third famous name in violin-making is Andreas Guarneri, who was a fellow pupil of Stradivarius.

Apart from being a superb craftsman, Stradivarius was said to have a secret – still unknown to this day – that allegedly made his violins sound sweeter, stronger, more resonant, than any others.

Stradivarius himself would no doubt be surprised to hear this since his 'secret' was probably no more mysterious than a painstaking skill in cutting and shaping his wood and adding many minor alterations and improvements to the existing models. Up to Stradivarius's time there was no standard shape for violins, makers still evolving their own ideas from the violin's predecessor, the viol. In those days – the end of the sixteenth century – the violin was a new instrument.

One of the secrets may have been the varnish that Stradivarius used to give his finished instruments their beautiful warm coloration varying between yellow and reddish brown. The formula for this varnish has been lost – nobody knows just how Stradivarius mixed it or exactly what ingredients went into it.

Modern violin makers, whilst admitting Stradivarius's mastery, are sceptical that he had any secret varnish. The varnish does not, they say, affect a violin's tone however much it may improve its appearance.

Stradivarius is known to have gone for long solitary walks in the high parts of the mountains where grew the trees from which he got his wood. It is now known that trees growing above a certain mountain line have a higher density of substance than those grown lower down. It may be, therefore, that Stradivarius's secret was his instinct for picking just the right tree.

He made violas and 'cellos as well as violins, and is known to have made guitars, one or two of which still survive.

Not only performers but collectors who cannot play a note value the Stradivarius instruments above all others. The Lady Anne Blunt Stradivarius (the instruments are named after their owners, or one-time owners, to distinguish them) was sold at Sothebys in London in 1971 for £84,000. Another Strad, known as the Messie, kept in the Ashmolean Museum at Oxford, has been theoretically valued for many years at £30,000 but its worth is probably nearer to £200,000.

How surprised Antonio Stradivarius would have been – if not totally unbelieving – to learn that his instruments, which he sold for a few shillings, could command such prodigious sums.

These prices depend partly on the magnificence of the instrument, partly on how much it has been played, partly on how perfect a condition it is in, and partly on how much some wealthy person wishes to own it.

But there are thousands of fakes, cheap instruments worth no more than a pound or two, although they bear inside a dusty-looking label reading *Antonius Stradivarius faciebat Cremonae* (made in Cremona) 1720. Many people have been bitterly disappointed at finding that some old instrument dug out of the attic, bearing the magic label, is in fact a worthless imitation.

The violin of today is very little different from that of Stradivarius's time. The pitch nowadays is higher, resulting in greater tension on the strings – 96lbs as against 63lbs – calling for the strengthening of certain parts; the compass of music having generally increased, the fingerboard has been extended to allow for the higher notes. But essentially the instrument is the same as those produced in Cremona and Brescia (another village in North Italy, famous for its violin makers) in the sixteenth and seventeenth centuries.

The next time you look at a violin – even if it is not a priceless 'Strad', note how its various parts have usefulness as well as beauty. Round the edge, for instance, you will see a thin thread of inlaid wood. This is not merely for decoration, but to prevent the fragile wood from splitting or cracking. The scroll (the carved piece just above the pegs), is useful for hanging up the instrument. The narrowed 'waist' facilitates the movement of the bow across the outer strings. The shape and position of the sound holes – usually called *f* holes from their shape – not only allow the sound to escape from the body, but help to balance the instrument.

24 Wagner – Composer to the Gods

Richard Wagner, born in 1813, was probably the worst-tempered man in our whole history – not excluding Beethoven, which is saying a lot. He has been described as the most unpleasant man of his time. He abused, lied about, and persecuted most of the people he met – particularly if they were Jewish. Anybody who behaved as he did, but lacked his towering talent, would undoubtedly have been shunned by everybody of his acquaintance.

His birth was a bit of a mystery. His mother was the widow of a policeman, who married an actor, who was possibly the boy's real father. Because of his step-father's profession, the young Wagner inevitably came into contact with the theatre from an early age. Both his mother and his step-father were cultivated, intelligent people and his forbears included a church musician and an author.

From boyhood days, Wagner was fascinated by the theatre, particularly the Greek theatre of ancient times. His earliest creative efforts were attempts at play-writing, a fact that was to have a considerable effect on his opera writing in later life.

His education was patchy, first at Dresden, then at Leipzig, finally at the Thomas School where Bach had been a student eighty years previously. He took lessons in composition and by nineteen had had a symphony performed in Prague.

Then followed a rather flat period. Wagner wrote and wrote (mostly operas), but with little success. As with so many young musicians, his advanced ideas and dismissal of the old way of doing things did not endear him to those in

A scene from Parsifal, *Wagner's last opera, produced in 1882*

authority who had the power to accept or reject his work.

To make a living he conducted at minor opera houses, no doubt getting more and more angry at having to conduct works that he felt were far inferior to his own.

In 1839, when he was twenty-six, he completed his best work to date – *Rienzi*, which was founded on a novel by Bulwer Lytton, the English historical writer.

Wagner wrote his own libretti (Italian for little books, the name given to the texts of operas and oratorios), partly because he rather fancied himself as a writer, but more because he felt that for opera to be truly successful, there had to be a total unity of words and music, and that the best person to accomplish this was the composer.

This view of Wagner's had a great effect on opera and for a long time it stood in his way, though eventually it was triumphantly successful and altered the whole pattern of opera writing. Another of his important points was the *leitmotiv* (German for leading motive),

Richard Wagner (1813-1883)

what we would call today the theme song, a melody or fragment of a melody constantly repeated or re-introduced to identify a character or situation. This device had been used before but Wagner made it an essential part of his Music Dramas, as he preferred to call them.

His originality and modernism, as well as his bad temper, made him very unpopular and for many years he was out in the cold.

Rienzi was rejected when he hopefully took it to Paris and tried to get a production for it there. He had to wait for three years until he could get someone to produce it in his home town of Dresden. But here it was a big success and secured for Wagner the musical directorship of the Dresden Court Opera a year later.

As soon as he got this appointment Wagner produced his second opera, *The Flying Dutchman*, and people began to sit up and take notice of this master talent. He began to gather important friends such as the young King Ludwig of Bavaria, and the famous philosopher Nietzsche, and Liszt, whose daughter Cosima he married.

Wagner now looked set for continuing success, and his production of *Tannhäuser* two years later seemed to confirm this. But he got mixed up in a political rebellion and had to flee the scenes of his successes. It was during this period that he entrusted the production of his next work, *Lohengrin*, to his friend Liszt, thereby making him a staunch supporter for life.

Then he went to Switzerland, where he spent eight years working on his giant *Ring of the Nibelung*, which took him twenty-five years to complete and takes four evenings to perform, and writing scores of books and pamphlets on his philosophical ideas. He also wrote *Tristan and Isolde*, which the Vienna opera abandoned after eighty rehearsals on the grounds that it was not performable (proved wrong by thousands of performances since).

At the age of sixty he embarked on the ambitious project of building his own theatre at Bayreuth, in Bavaria, in order that his Music Dramas could be presented the way he wanted. Funds were subscribed from all over the world and four years later the Festival Theatre received its triumphant opening. It is still there today and still running Wagnerian festivals.

25 The Romantic Opera

Guiseppe Verdi (1813-1901)

Opera really started in Italy and it was only in after years that giants like Wagner arose in other countries. Despite this, Italy remained the home of a more romantic type of opera, of which Guiseppe Verdi was a master.

Verdi's operas, unlike Wagner's gloomy masterpieces, were warm and human, telling tales that were within the grasp of everyone.

Born in the same year as Wagner, Verdi had a completely different background. He was born in a humble cottage in a village near Parma, North Italy, the son of peasants. His education was meagre but even at the earliest age he showed a talent for music and he was urged to try for a scholarship at the Milan Conservatoire of Music. This he did, only to be turned down for 'insufficient talent!'

Fortunately for him, a wealthy amateur musician was so impressed by his ability that he paid for his education. Thus the two joint masters of opera – Wagner and Verdi – went their almost identical ways at almost exactly the same time; Wagner to study at Leipzig, Verdi at Milan.

Very soon the 'insufficient talent' began to produce the first signs of the master composer. By his twenties Verdi had written his first two operas; these attracted no great attention, being little more than the tentative promises of brilliant work to come.

Verdi's first break came when he was twenty-five. His opera *Nebuchadnezzar* smashed through the opposition and declared the arrival of a new and vigorous young personality. It was produced at the prestigous La Scala Opera House in Milan.

Although *Nebuchadnezzar* was on a biblical theme, there were political overtones in it which delighted the Italian audiences. Just about this time the Italians were getting very restive about Austrian rule over the northern provinces of Italy – a strong surge of patriotism which was eventually to lead to the unification of Italy under King Victor Emanuel.

Verdi of course knew all about this and was as fiercely partisan as any but, whether subconsciously or deliberately, he contrived to get into his operas a feeling of more or less open hatred for the foreign oppressor. In a string of operas, produced and presented at the rate of one a year, he put over this idea until he was the hero of the public. *The Lombards at the First Crusade* (1843), *Ernana* (after a story by Victor Hugo, 1844), *Joan of Arc* (1845), *Attila the Hun* (1846), *Macbeth* (1847) and *The Battle of Legnano* (1849) were some of the works he poured out with ever increasing skill.

Apart from the opportunism of these patriotic operas, they displayed a great gift of melody, masterly use of the orchestra and an exceptional gift for drawing character studies in musical terms. These talents began to spread Verdi's fame in countries where the patriotic message had little or no appeal.

Perceiving this, Verdi switched to stories of a wider interest. *Rigoletto* (based on another Victor Hugo novel, *The King Amuses Himself*) was a huge success in Venice, London and New York. Verdi immediately followed it up with *Il Trovatore* (The Troubadour), which was also a worldwide success, being produced in New

York in the same year as *Rigoletto* (1855). The third masterpiece of this period was *La Traviata* (The Woman Led Astray), another worldwide hit, which Verdi took only three months to write.

By now wealthy and famous, Verdi began to ease off. Opera houses were coming to him and begging for works.

Aida was produced in Cairo (then under French influence) in 1871, when Verdi was fifty-eight and undisputed master of the Italian opera. Had he but known it, however, there was a thirteen-year-old boy, just about to enter Milan Conservatoire, who was watching the master and planning to take over from him.

Giacomo Puccini was one of the fifth generation of musicians to hold official posts in Italy. By the time the young man reached his early twenties he was already writing operas and submitting them to publishers and competitions. One of these caught the attention of the head of the great firm of Milan music publishers, Ricordi's.

This was a young man's work and owed as

much to Verdi as it did to Wagner. But the publisher recognised true talent beneath the imitation and encouraged the young man over a long period of nine years until he struck his true form with *Manon Lescaut* (1893), which immediately established his fame and fortune. He followed it with *La Bòheme* (The Bohemian), *Madame Butterfly*, *Tosca* – all of them worldwide hits. He was hailed as the new master of Italian opera.

Verdi, however, was far from being knocked off his throne. At the age of seventy-three he produced *Otello*, an undoubted masterpiece. As if this were not enough, Verdi produced, in his eightieth year, a new *opera buffa* (comedy opera) *Falstaff*, so full of fun and vitality that it might have been written by a man a quarter of Verdi's age. What is more it showed an astonishingly modern development of style and method, reflecting Wagner's influence. It was as if the

production and huge success of Puccini's *Manon Lescaut* had stung the old man into reply; as if he had said to the bustling newcomer 'You can't have the crown yet, I'm still using it'.

And he was, too. In his eighty-fifth year he produced his *Ave Maria* and *Stabat Mater*. He lasted, vital and vigorous, until he was eighty-eight.

Meanwhile, Puccini was going from success to success. America loved his work and it was during a visit there that Puccini got fascinated with the cowboy idiom and produced an opera with the modern-sounding title of *The Girl of the Golden West*. Puccini's last opera, *Turandot*, was to be a grand affair on a Chinese theme, full of drama and spectacle – perhaps he had been stung by Verdi's dismissal of him as a 'lightweight'. But he never lived to complete it, that being done by another Italian composer, Franco Alfano. It was first produced in 1926.

A scene from Verdi's opera Aïda, *one of his most popular works*

Peter Ilich Tchaikovsky (1840-1892)

26 Tchaikovsky – Master of the Ballet

When Wagner died in 1883 he had dominated European music – Germany, France, Italy and England had all felt his influence. But not Russia.

Russian composers had travelled to Europe and heard Wagner's music but it meant very little to them. A month before Wagner's death, their leading composer, Tchaikovsky, had heard Wagner's *Tristan and Isolde* opera and reported that 'he had never been so bored in all his life'.

Why Western music had never really taken root in Russia is unknown – possibly because the aristocratic world of Russia was a closed one, impervious to outside happenings and making up its own standards.

Peter Ilich Tchaikovsky was a typical product of this world, although he was to spread his influence far outside his native country.

He started out to be a civil servant and studied for that calling. He was a young man before he came to the conclusion that music was the only thing that really interested him and he enrolled as a student in the St. Petersburg Conservatoire. There he studied under Anton Rubinstein, the great Russian pianist and composer, who had founded the Conservatoire in 1862 and who wrote twenty operas, six symphonies, five piano concertos and a host of other music; but who is remembered today mostly because of one of his trifles – the haunting *Melody in F*.

At this time Russian music was dominated by a group of Russian composers calling themselves The Five – Balakiref, Cui, Borodin, Mussorgsky and Rimsky-Korsakov. They were all about the same age as Tchaikovsky but formed an inner circle to which he did not really belong.

Nevertheless he was much influenced by them and his famous *Romeo and Juliet* overture-fantasia was not only dedicated to Balakiref but its first draft was written under his guidance. The Five wrote off Wagner and Brahms and so Tchaikovsky did too.

But he was a solitary, emotion-torn man. He married a girl and left her immediately; he carried out a passionate correspondence with an older woman who he never met but who became his lifelong financial benefactress.

Like most great composers, Tchaikovsky had his eccentric moments and it is said that he paused in the middle of writing his Fourth Symphony to write a long letter to his woman patroness explaining that the symphony represented Fate and was to be treated as such. Nobody ever knew whether he was pulling her leg or not but it was the fashionable practice of the time to say that every important piece of music represented something, so perhaps Tchaikovsky was merely giving his music some 'meaning' before it was too late.

He was certainly not averse to trying out new ideas. In his delicate *Dance of the Sugar Plum Fairy* from his *Nutcracker* ballet he used the celesta, in 1892 a brand new instrument, with startling effect.

Tchaikovsky's spreading fame did not always impress or please his colleagues. Indeed, Nicholas

Rubinstein, the brother of Tchaikovsky's teacher Anton, considerably shocked Tchaikovsky when he refused to play the B Flat Minor Piano Concerto, dedicated to himself, on the grounds that it was not good enough.

Tchaikovsky wrote ten operas (*Eugene Onegin*, *The Queen of Spades*), six symphonies (*Pathetic*), three ballets (*Nutcracker*, *Swan Lake*, *Sleeping Beauty*), and of course the famous *1812 Overture* complete with cannons, church bells, national anthems and the noise of Napoleon's armies being repulsed by the gallant Russian soldiers.

His original idea was to perform this vast, noisy but exciting work in a public square in Moscow, complete with a huge orchestra, a brass band, the cathedral's carillon of bells, and a goodly detachment of artillery!

Perhaps because of this kind of showmanship, music critics are apt to underestimate Tchaikovsky's talents. As long ago as the 1890s George Bernard Shaw, then a music critic, wrote that Tchaikovsky 'had a thoroughly Byronic power of being tragic, momentous, romantic, about nothing at all'.

Tchaikovsky's overture 1812 *commemorated Napoleon's retreat from Moscow after his defeat*

27 The Last Romantics

chorus of 400, a grand organ and 130 orchestral instruments, including harmonium and mandoline, and it lasted for an hour and forty minutes. Mahler was conductor of the Vienna Philarmonic Orchestra and a pupil of Bruckner.

By the end of the nineteenth century, music in the form of opera, ballet and orchestral recitals was a major form of entertainment. The music hall, with the singers of ballads and comic songs, was a favourite entertainment for those who found the concert hall too heavy going for them. Ballroom dancing was an accepted pastime and family music in the Victorian and Edwardian home was one of the features of domestic life. Vienna, because of its illustrious background, was still held by many to be the musical capital of Europe, and the great end-of-century composers in Vienna were Johannes Brahms, Gustav Mahler and Anton Bruckner.

Brahms was the son of the double bass player in the Hamburg theatre orchestra and got off to a good start with a first-class musical training as a boy. By the time he was twenty he had attracted the notice and appreciation of Franz Liszt, who helped him considerably in his career, as did Robert Schumann. For a time he earned his living in the court of a minor German noble, but by the time he was thirty he had settled in Vienna, the city that was to make his fame and fortune. There he wrote four symphonies, two piano concertos and a host of other fine music.

Bruckner, a schoolmaster until he was 30, flourished in Vienna at the same time as Brahms, producing nine symphonies, three masses and many other works. He was well-known in London for his organ recitals. He was rather solemn and so was his music. He could not resist tinkering with it once it was finished, six of his symphonies exist in two or three different versions.

The third of the trio, Mahler, was more of a rebel. He liked to shake audiences with startling innovations. He wrote symphonies for huge orchestras and vast choirs. One of them, the 8th Symphony in E flat, *Symphony of a Thousand*, called for eight soloists, double chorus, a boys'

A scene from Mussorgsky's opera, Boris Godounof, *of which there were five different versions*

78

In Prague there were Smetana, whose opera *The Bartered Bride* is still very popular, and Dvořák, whose *New World Symphony*, written in New York, was an important forerunner of the changes to come. Dvořák started life as a butcher's boy and lived in direst poverty while he studied music, first becoming a viola player in a Prague theatre before going on to world fame as a composer and the head of the New York Conservatoire.

Gustav Mahler (1860-1911)

Claude Debussy (1862-1918)

In Paris Debussy was writing his dream-like music, *Prélude à L'Après Midi d'un Faune* and *La Mer* among many other works that began to challenge the old ways of musical harmony.

In London, the son of a Worcester organist and music seller, a violin teacher named Edward Elgar was writing the master work which was to lead him on to wealth, fame and a knighthood: the *Engima Variations*. The full title of this is *Variations on an Original Theme*, but the theme itself is never heard. Elgar said the fourteen variations were musical portraits of himself and thirteen friends, whose initials appear at the head of each section. One of his *Pomp and Circumstance* marches, (*Land of Hope and Glory*) became so popular that he became quite irritable when asked to conduct it, believing that it overshadowed his more important works.

What has come to be known as the Classical Period had begun a hundred years previously with the passing of Bach and Handel. The composers' patrons then were princes and noblemen at whose courts they worked. C. P. E. Bach, son of the great Johann Sebastian Bach, was one of the originators of the sonata form (a sonata is a work in two or three movements for a solo instrument with accompaniment, often including a dance movement such as a minuet); Haydn developed the symphony; Mozart specialised in instrumental and operatic writing of unsurpassed beauty; Schubert developed the art of lieder (poetic songs) to its highest level.

Johannes Brahms (1833-1897)

Anton Bruckner (1824-1884)

Frederick Smetana (1824-1884)

These and others were the great classicists. Inevitably, there was a reaction. The new school said the music was too perfect, it lacked feeling and expression.

Led by Schubert with his romantic lieder and Beethoven with his symphonies, a new style came into vogue, in which feeling was all important and the expressing of emotion became the prime aim of musical composition. This was called the Romantic Period and it leaned heavily on literature for its themes, even borrowing from actual events like Napoleon's retreat from Moscow and illustrating it with cannons and church bells interwoven with the music, as in the famous Tchaikovsky *1812 Overture*. Liszt introduced the idea of writing some sentences at the beginning of his compositions explaining what they were about – he called this 'programme music', as distinct from 'abstract' or 'absolute music', which expressed nothing at all except beautiful sounds. Weber, Mendelssohn, Chopin and Liszt were the great men of the orchestral Romantic Period. Wagner, Charles Francois Gounod, Georges Bizet, Hector Berlioz, Verdi and Puccini founded and developed Romantic Opera.

But the day of the Romantics was drawing to its close. At the end of the nineteenth century the voices of the new breed of composers were heard, impatient with the old and anxious to take over and have done with what they felt was the sticky sentimentality of the Romantics.

Anton Dvořák (1841-1904)

81

28 Ballads, Songs and Snatches

Writing at much the same time as Tchaikovsky, though on a very different plane, were the famous English pair, Gilbert and Sullivan.

As a young man, Sullivan went to Leipzig on a scholarship to study music, wrote a symphony and other serious works, but it was not until he met Gilbert and collaborated with him on a long series of light operas that success really came his way.

He and Gilbert made a perfect team although they quarrelled often. Gilbert wrote amusing verses about happenings of the time and Sullivan composed rather catchy music to fit even the most difficult verbal rhythms.

Their long series of successes at the Savoy Theatre: *The Mikado, The Gondoliers, Trial by Jury, Iolanthe, The Pirates of Penzance, Yeomen of the Guard* and others, made them wealthy and famous. Sullivan still desired to write more serious music, however, and one of the best of his other works was an oratorio based on Longfellow's poem *The Golden Legend*. Queen Victoria liked his music and knighted him in 1883.

This did not please his partner at all. Gilbert thought he was equally deserving of a knighthood. But he had to wait until 1908, seven years after Sullivan's death before he got his wish. Four years later he was drowned while bathing in an ornamental lake in the grounds of his home in Harrow Weald.

82

A scene from The Mikado, *by Gilbert and Sullivan, produced in more than a dozen languages*

29 The Rebels

Already, at the end of the nineteenth century, there were the first rumblings of a musical revolution. Dvořák, Debussy, Ravel and others were challenging the old concepts and producing music that was considered masterly by some but merely peculiar by others. They were the first to try to shake off the pattern laid down by the classical masters.

But waiting in the wings, so to speak, were three young men who were determined not merely to shake the pillars of well-ordered classicism but to pull down the whole structure and start again on entirely new lines.

The first of these was Arnold Schönberg, born in Vienna in 1874, and earning his living as an orchestrator of theatre music and conductor of theatre orchestras. By his early thirties, however, he shattered the musical world with his 'atonal' music. ('Atonal' means having no key – the notes are totally unrelated by any of the laws of harmony built up so painstakingly over the centuries.) Other composers had toyed experimentally with this idea of atonality, but it took the wayward brilliance of Schönberg to turn mere theory into shatteringly powerful music.

To the inexperienced ear, atonal music sounds dreadful, just musical chaos and disorder.

But there is method in it – a theory that the composer, if he is to express himself fully, must not be restricted by rules or tied down by tradition.

Schönberg extended this even to the formation of the orchestra. He discarded completely the standard orchestral line-up used by the great composers, with its families of instruments, its balanced groups of strings, woodwind, brass and percussion. One of Schönberg's most remarkable compositions, *Pierrot Lunaire*, used one female voice, piano, flute, clarinet, violin, 'cello and introduced 'speech-song'. Schönberg's most important contribution to music was his 'twelve-note' technique, in which a set pattern of the notes of the chromatic scale are used and re-used in various forms. The more developed form of this kind of music is called serialism.

In general the public and critics hated the new music. His symphony, *Peleas and Melisande*, which called for three choirs, an orchestra of 155, several teams of solo singers, and specially printed 65-stave score paper, sounded to many like demented sawing, scraping, banging and wailing. One critic wrote: 'It's not only full of wrong notes but is a fifty-minute wrong note itself'.

But others felt that Schönberg was progressing towards a completely new idea in music – producing violent reactions by sound. 'Away with the old ideas,' cried Schönberg, 'let's try something – anything – that is new.'

He soon attracted admirers and adherents to his ideas. One of his pupils, Alban Berg, eleven years younger than his master, was rather less way out, and tried to combine the twelve-note technique with the older forms. His compositions have been described as being 'filled with dark melancholy and lacerating anguish'. His most outstanding work was the opera *Wozzeck*, which tells the story of a soldier who is betrayed by the woman he loves, murders her then drowns himself in a pond while their child plays innocently at the water edge. Not exactly a cheerful story but written with such compelling force that the power of the music transcends the sordid and depressing story. Berg uses every kind of music style and mixes them up until the listener is bewildered.

Berg's other masterpiece was a violin concerto, dedicated to Mahler's step-daughter, which went a long way towards bridging the gap between the old tonal system of writing and the new atonality.

Another pupil of Schönberg's was Anton von Webern, nine years younger than Schönberg and very soon regarding his master as rather traditional. Not only did he completely abandon any trace of recognised harmonic structure but almost everything else as well – including length. His *Three Small Pieces* for 'cello and piano are rightly named, for the second of the *Pieces* lasts for only ten seconds, and the third is only ten

Arnold Schönberg (1847-1951)

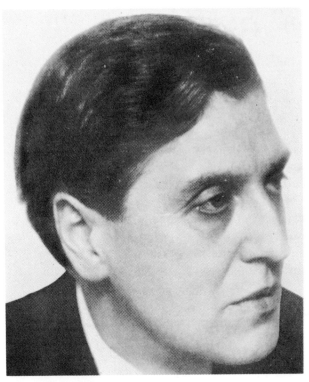

Alban Berg (1885-1935)

Anton von Webern (1883-1945)

Alexander Scriabin (1872-1915)

bars long and has eight notes for the 'cello and twelve for the piano.

His end was as dramatic as his music. While smoking a last late evening cigarette near his home in Salzburg, Austria, one night in 1945, he was accidentally shot by an American sentry.

Correction
Caption should read (top left):
Arnold Schönberg (1874-1951)

30 Stravinsky – the Frontiersman

While Schönberg was pioneering in Vienna, another young man, sixteen at the time, was thinking the same thoughts in St. Petersburg.

His father was a singer in the opera and made his son study law, but his heart was always in music. By the age of twenty he had got his way and had begun his belated study of the subject under Rimsky-Korsakov during the two years prior to the latter's death.

In his middle twenties Igor Stravinsky met a remarkable man, Serge Diaghilef, the creator of the famous Russian Ballet Company. Diaghilef, besides being a gifted impresario and controller of wild temperaments, believed in the new music. Stravinsky fell instantly under his spell and produced a string of masterpieces for him.

The first of these was *Firebird* and its performance in Paris in 1910, when Stravinsky was twenty-eight, not only produced uproar among the critics but made Stravinsky into a celebrity overnight. A year later he produced *Petrushka*, which set the seal on his international fame to such an extent that he was cut off from his native Russia for the rest of his life. He became a French citizen in 1934 and an American citizen in 1945, where he lived in Beverley Hills among the film stars in Hollywood.

In 1913 Stravinsky produced *The Rite of Spring*, which caused a riot – the critics called it 'destruction of music . . . barbarism . . . noise'. But Stravinsky went steadily on, unmoved by these hard words. He used a huge orchestra for *The Rite of Spring* but the whistles and catcalls that greeted the first night performance made the orchestra almost inaudible. The next work, however, used only four pianos and percussion.

When the First World War came, Stravinsky returned for a brief visit to Russia but found himself completely out of touch with his native country and so took up residence in Switzerland. But times were hard – the war had dried up Stravinsky's income from his property in Russia and there was no ballet. Stravinsky started to write works which could be played by small groups – *Ragtime*, for ten instruments and percussion, and *The Soldier's Tale* for only seven instruments (clarinet, bassoon, cornet, trombone, violin, double bass and percussion). His idea was that a small company could travel from village to village. But the latter was performed only once during the war and it was only in later years that it became well-known.

After the war Stravinsky renewed contact with Diaghilef, writing *Pulcinella*, a ballet based on some fragments of music by the eighteenth-century Italian composer Pergolesi.

At the age of seventy, Stravinsky startled the musical world by a complete switch in composing style. At first he had been a leader in advanced ideas but the years had mellowed him to a style which, although aggressive and modern, was still easy to take by those who wanted something more challenging than the classics. Then, suddenly he abandoned this in favour of something that was a good deal more like Schönberg or Webern.

Stravinsky's new style was based on what is called 'serialism' – that is, musical composition built on a fixed series of notes, rather than letting the imagination contrive any sequence at will. It is a very complicated subject and imposes on its users an extremely difficult set of conditions. The octave is divided into twelve steps, which can be placed in any order the composer fancies. This series may be used at any pitch but all twelve notes must be used before any of them can be repeated, and so on. There are many more rules and the whole thing seems to some people to be a kind of elaborate puzzle just to make composing more difficult. But the master composers can produce master composi- tions whatever the rules, and Stravinsky's experiments with the twelve-note scale have produced some remarkable effects.

Stravinsky's big cantata, *Threni*, is based entirely on the twelve-note scale and is bare and entirely free of the exuberances and excitements of his youthful work.

Stravinsky always surprised other musicians. Even when he was only writing instructions for the musicians he nearly always did something different. In 1923, when he published his *Octet for Wind Instruments* he expressly forbade the use of *diminuendo* or *crescendo* in the playing of the work – so that the structure would be more clearly brought out!

The young Stravinsky meets the famous ballet impresario, Diaghilef, in Paris

31 The Twentieth Century

Our story of music, although by no means finished, is nearly up to date. As we look around us in the mid-twentieth century, what do we find?

The great master works, some of which have been mentioned in these pages, are still being performed and admired all over the world, even in those countries like China, Japan and India which came late to Western music and its ideas of composition and harmony.

The names of the writers of the great master works are familiar to most people, even to those who profess no great interest in music. Such has been their impact on the world that it would be impossible to compile a list of those who have influenced men's minds without including many of them.

And the moderns are so well established that resistance to their music has very largely subsided. The 'shocking noises' of Stravinsky are now accepted without difficulty.

In Hungary, Béla Bartók wrote powerful and discordant music which is much played today. Bartok, who was born in the Torontal district of Hungary, now Rumania, in 1881, lived until 1945 when he died in New York. As a young composer in Budapest he was fiercely and angrily resisted by the more conservative musicians of that city, although he was made professor of the Academy at twenty-six. All his life he suffered from bad health, and his childhood was one long succession of illnesses. But with the aid of his mother (a school teacher), enough money was scraped up to pay for his musical education. But his real passion was the folk music of his country – he did not believe that the noisy flashy so-called Hungarian gypsy music was the true folk music, and he spent a large part of his life tracking down what he believed to be the real thing, travelling many thousands of miles in the mountains of the Balkans, recording the music on a primitive wax-cylinder phonograph. Folk music was the basis for most of his

Béla Bartók (1881-1953)

compositions. He wrote mostly for strings and piano but departed from his normal practice long enough to write a clarinet concerto (*Contrasts*), for Benny Goodman, the King of Swing, in the 1930s.

In Russia there were several outstanding moderns. Prokofiev (1891–1953) had started his career before the Russian revolution but came to terms with it, returning to that country after having lived abroad for a while. His music is dry and spiky, with more than a little sense of humour. Although he has written many concertos, sonatas and ballets, he will probably be best remembered for his children's piece, *Peter and the Wolf*, using narrator and orchestra.

Another Russian 'modern' is Shostakovich, born in 1906, who became famous overnight with his first symphony, written when he was nineteen. Shostakovich has suffered his ups and downs, at one time being described as the 'composer laureate' of the Soviet Union, but a few years later he was in disgrace as 'bourgeois in temperament'. But whatever his reputation in these respects, there is no doubt that he is one of the world's major living composers.

Aram Khachaturian, an Armenian born in Tiflis in 1903, also suffered the switchbacks of Russian esteem and condemnation. In 1939 he received the Order of Lenin and four years later his name was enshrined on a marble plaque in the hall of Moscow Conservatoire. But five years later he was publicly reproved, together with Prokofiev and Shostakovich, for 'vicious, anti-popular, and formalist trends and bourgeois ideology'. But Khachaturian is enormously gifted and not at all afraid to experiment. In his *Piano Concerto*, for instance, he uses a flexatone (a jazz instrumental toy of the 1930s which has a metal tongue beaten by two wooden hammers resulting in a whining sliding noise like a musical saw).

In France there is Darius Milhaud (born 1892) a member of The Six, a group of modernist Parisian composers who dominated the scene after the First World War with their sparkling dissonant music. Arthur Honegger (1892–1955)

and Francis Poulenc (1899–1963) also belonged to The Six, who were completed by the lesser-known Tailleferre, Durey and Georges Auric. Their music carried such challenging titles as *Perpetual Motion, The Ox on the Roof, The Bores* and jointly they declared war on Wagner and all his works. Milhaud went on to more serious things with his ambitious modernistic opera *Christophe Colomb*, and Honegger became famous for his tone poem *Pacific 231*, which set out to convey the effect of an American locomotive.

Seldom in this book has Spain been mentioned. That is because she contributed no major composers to music until the twentieth century, her music having been in eclipse since her collapse as a major power in the seventeenth century. But Manuel de Falla (1876–1946) and

LEFT: *Serge Prokofiev (1891-1953)*

RIGHT: *Paul Hindemith (1895-1963)*

*Béla Bartók recording Hungarian folk music on
his primitive phonograph in the early 1900s*

Isaac Albéniz (1860–1909) did much to re-establish their country musically. Falla's best known work is probably *Nights in the Gardens of Spain*, and Albéniz, who was a brilliant pianist and pupil of Liszt, wrote more than 250 pieces for piano as well as three operas. One of the oddities of the piano pieces is how they contrive to make the piano sound like a guitar. Falla's *Three Cornered Hat* ballet was commissioned by the famous Diaghilef for his Russian Ballet and became a modern classic. Falla never lived to fulfill his brilliant promise; he was drowned when the ship he was travelling on was torpedoed by a German submarine.

It is rare that governments take such an interest in music as to award a state salary to a composer just so that he can go on composing without the necessity for having to worry about making a living. This was the good fortune of Jean Sibelius, the Finnish composer. He studied in Berlin and Vienna but went back to live in Finland and quickly became recognised as a composer of world stature. Sibelius lived to be ninety but his great work *Finlandia*, a symphonic poem based on national Finnish themes, will live a great deal longer.

Paul Hindemith, born in Germany in 1895, left home at the age of eleven to make a career as a musician. By fifteen he was leader of the orchestra at Frankfurt Opera; by his middle twenties he announced that the disorder created by Schönberg, Webern and Berg and all that lot would be ruthlessly swept away and tidied up. He thought 'art for art's sake' was a lot of nonsense and that the composer was there to do a utilitarian job of entertaining the public. This was not quite such bombastic nonsense as it might sound but derived largely from the back history of music when much fine music was written strictly to order for the pleasure of noble patrons.

But alas for Hindemith, his public seemed indifferent to his many outpourings. He was a prolific composer, writing anything and everything from jazz to symphonies. But it was not until the Nazis came to power in Germany, and made it clear that the public was not going to have much say in anything, that Hindemith threw off his self-imposed 'please-the-public' role and started to write music to please himself.

But although the quality of his music increased greatly, his personal success did not. He made the mistake of writing an opera, *Mathis the Painter*, that contained the idea that the creative artist must not be fettered by government control. The Nazis banned the opera and Hindemith left hurriedly for Turkey. After re-organising Turkish musical life on Western lines, he left to tour America and settled there in 1939. He returned to Europe, having been head of Yale University Musical Department for eleven years, to take up a similar post at Zurich. He died in 1963.

Looking further afield, one name which must be mentioned is that of Villa Lobos, of Brazil. Although such a long way from the musical centres of Europe, Villa Lobos was an international figure, pouring out compositions of all types, at a quite prodigious rate. It is almost impossible to keep track of his output, since he would dash off anything from a simple piece for solo guitar to a studied work for chorus and large orchestra.

Using the material ready to hand, Villa Lobos' music has a strong local flavour, being often based on Brazilian folk music and using the percussion instruments made familiar to everyone by Latin American rumba bands. One of his most popular items is a 'musical picture' called *The Little Train*.

One of the problems in writing about mid-century music is that it changes and develops so quickly that almost anything one can say is out of date almost as soon as the ink is dry.

It took several thousand years for music to get as far as the simple plainsong of the Middle Ages; from there it took another three hundred years to develop polyphony (many sounds); another three hundred years or so has spanned the greats of music from Bach to Beethoven; from Beethoven to now is so crammed with names, music and happenings that it is almost impossible to list them.

Thus, by the 1950s–1970s there is a bewildering variety of music to listen to, to explore and to think about. Not only is there the great mass of fine music from the past, but an ever increasing modern output. Furthermore, musicians continually explore new ways of making music, new thoughts about what music is.

We have touched briefly in an earlier chapter on the musical idea called 'serialism' – the basing of music on a fixed succession of notes. This would undoubtedly have seemed not only totally unnecessary but totally mad to the composers of an earlier age. And yet some of the finest musical minds of the mid-twentieth century are fascinated by it.

The twelve notes of the twelve-note scale are capable of being arranged in over 479,000,000 different ways – enough to last out the longest composition without repetition. Pierre Boulez, a leading exponent of this kind of music, wrote a work for two pianos called *Structures*, with the note values of one piano worked out on twelve different lengths, while the second piano plays an inversion of the same rhythmic values. The work lasts for ninety pages. Other composers have organised all the other parts of music (expression marks, instrumentation, metronome speeds and so on) in a similar arithmetical way.

The remarkable thing about all this calculation is that some very impressive music has come out of it – not really comparable to a Bach fugue or a Beethoven symphony, but exciting and sometimes moving. But there are some signs that this 'brain music' has gone as far as it can and that its advocates are turning back to the more ordinary forms.

Others are not content to stop at serialism but try to push experiments even further. There is, for instance, the school of thought which denies the necessity for any strict organisation at all.

The German composer Stockhausen (born 1928) in his work *Zeitmässe*, gave five wind instruments a few notes with instructions to play them in their own time and as they wish, with the conductor (yes, there is a conductor!) merely bringing them together at certain points. In another work, *Groups for Three Orchestras*, the orchestras are conducted separately at different speeds by three conductors.

The American, John Cage (born in Los Angeles 1912), uses a prepared piano which adds such things as screws, bolts, hairpins, bits of wood and so on to the strings and thus produces a series of bangs, thumps and buzzes rather than notes of definite pitch, the work as often as not finishing with a grand slam of the

Dmitri Shostakovich (1906-19   )

piano lid. Cage was a pupil of Schönberg and a follower of the Italian Marinetti (1876–1944) who advocated the use of noise makers of all kinds in music. Marinetti gave recitals in Rome, Paris, London and elsewhere which as often as not resulted in the audience hurling vegetables, eggs and other 'noise makers' at the stage. He was created a Senator by Mussolini and put in charge of the cultural side of Fascism.

There is almost no limit to the lengths such experimental music can go. One composer produced his works by holding music manuscript paper up to the light, observing where imperfections in the paper occured, and writing notes near the markings.

Whether all this kind of thing can be called music at all is open to doubt. But before it is dismissed as mere fakery or leg-pulling, it is as well to remember what the critics said about Wagner's opera – 'dog music – sick noises' – and about Stravinsky – 'destruction of music – barbarism – noise.' Yet today Wagner's music is accepted without question and Stravinsky's is regarded as rather old-fashioned.

It is right that there should be experiments and inevitable that some of the experiments are

Aram Khachaturian (1903-19   )

Jean Sibelius (1865-1951)

an absurd waste of time. But to ban all experiment would be to sound the death knell of music, for experiments have been going on for centuries – ever since the daring idea of singing two different notes at the same time was tried out in the seventh century. Or since primitive man first twanged the string of his bow and discovered that putting one end of the bow in his mouth made the sound louder.

But if serialism seems to have gone as far as it can, there are certainly other forms of experimentation going on. The invention of electronic instruments, including the tape recorder, opened up a huge new field of music making. This is such an important subject that it is dealt with separately in another chapter.

There is no doubt that music in the mid-twentieth century is rich, full, alive and exciting. The superb music of the past centuries is in no danger of being forgotten but it is being added to by new composers writing not only in the old traditions but in new areas still only partly explored.

The rise of popular music, too, should not be overlooked. There always has been popular music – music outside the church and the concert

hall. Inevitably it has been simple music, but it had tremendous drive and appeal. There have been periods in history when it has been shunned by the church as 'wicked' and other times when the church has happily borrowed from it and incorporated it in its own music.

The mid-century finds these two forms of music getting closer and closer together. Talented musicians of international stature such as Leonard Bernstein, recognised as one of the top symphony orchestra conductors of today, quite happily write Broadway musicals containing hit songs that make the Top Ten in most countries.

Sir William Walton, one of the greatest living British composers, writes music for films. Andre Previn, conductor of the London Symphony Orchestra, is a firstclass jazz pianist. Swing clarinettist Benny Goodman commissioned a work from Béla Bartók and recorded the Mozart clarinet concerto.

Perhaps the most important thing about mid-century music is that the gulf between popular music and serious music gets narrower and narrower. Perhaps there is only good music and bad music – and ever the twain shall meet.

32 Music in Britain

Britain, at one time thought to be backward in producing great musicians, came very much into the forefront in this century with men like Ralph Vaughan Williams, Arthur Bliss, Gustav Holst (British of Swedish descent) with his oft-played *Planets Suite*, and Frederick Delius.

More recent are Sir William Walton, Alan Rawsthorne, Sir Benjamin Britten, Sir Michael Tippett, Sir Arnold Bax, Edmund Rubbra, Lennox Berkeley (a pupil of the gifted French-woman, Nadia Boulenger).

It is not necessary to dig very far into history to see that England has always had an inventive and scholarly past. There was, for example, the famous organ built at the monastery in Winchester which was the wonder of the musical world in AD 980, and needed seventy men to blow it. Then there was the new way of singing church music, in sixths and thirds, invented in the thirteenth century and widely adopted throughout European church music, called 'English descant'.

John Dunstable (1380–1453) had a great reputation throughout Europe and, following the victories in France of Henry V, went to that country to teach the French musicians the

English style of writing which was much in advance of anything else at that time.

The Three T's of sixteenth century Tudor times had a great influence on music when all was in confusion due to the transition from the Church of Rome to the Church of England. John Taverner was a master of polyphony and used it to write for a consort of viols (group of bowed string instruments) in an entirely new way. Christopher Tye was a Doctor of Music of both Oxford and Cambridge Universities and wrote many fine anthems. Thomas Tallis was the founder of English cathedral music and composed much good church music including a remarkable piece for forty voices and eight choruses. Tallis's pupil, William Byrd, was comparable in stature to the great Palestrina.

This period has been called the Golden Age of English music and certainly there were some outstanding talents in the service of church music. But it was also a great period for secular (non-religious) music. Henry VIII was a tolerably good composer; his daughter Elizabeth played the virginals and encouraged music and musicians. Music was a part of family life – singing madrigals (compositions for four or more voices on gay themes) and accompanying them on viols, virginals and lutes was one of the great

A scene from Benjamin Britten's opera Peter Grimes, *first produced in London 1945*

entertainments of the times and the skills, both in writing the works and in performing them, reached a very high level.

John Dowland was a virtuoso player of the lute and a composer of no small merit. He travelled Europe like a star and was made much of at the courts of Charles I of England and Christian IV of Denmark. He was able to boast of having his lute music published in eight different capitals. Other English musicians followed his example in travelling abroad and were much esteemed. One of them, with the appropriate name of John Bull, became cathedral organist at Antwerp and wrote a piece that was the forerunner of the British National Anthem.

During Cromwellian times (middle 1600s), although music was banned from the churches by the Puritans, it flourished elsewhere and even Cromwell himself had a staff organist for special occasions and as tutor for his daughter. And, even though the Puritans had also closed the theatres, the first English opera, *The Siege of Rhodes*, was produced at this time (1656).

In 1659 was born one of the truly great English composers, Henry Purcell. He wrote an opera (*Dido*), masques, church music, songs and music for strings. One famous piece that Purcell did not write is that which is erroneously called 'Purcell's *Trumpet Voluntary*', the true title of which is *The Prince of Denmark's March* and which was written by Jeremiah Clarke.

When we come to the 1700s we encounter the famous Dr Thomas Arne, the outstanding composer of his time. His best work was *Comus*, a setting of the Milton masque, but his most famous work is undoubtedly *Rule Britannia*, which came in the masque *Alfred*, presented at Drury Lane in 1749.

That England was not backward with orchestral music is demonstrated by the many large orchestral and vocal performances mounted towards the end of the eighteenth century. Haydn was given a London orchestra of sixty players, more than he had ever had in his life before, and the Handel Commemoration in 1784 had an orchestra which included ninety-five violins, twenty-six oboes and twenty-six bassoons. These massed orchestras were the beginning of the still-operating Three Choirs Festivals.

Song writing, too, was flourishing and many

famous songs survive from that day – *The British Grenadiers, Down Among the Dead Men, The Vicar of Bray* and *The Roast Beef of Old England*, to name but a few.

The nineteenth century was dominated by visiting foreign geniuses and their works. Handel at the end of the previous century, became as English as any of them and was buried in Westminster Abbey. He was followed by Haydn (who said 'A good deal of my symphonies must be altered to suit English tastes'), the Mozart family, Wagner (in 1855 as conductor of the Philharmonic Society's concerts), Mendelssohn (1836 and 1846, conducting his own oratorios) and Chopin (who is said to have taken his nocturne style from the Irish pianist and composer, John Field). Rossini (who earned the then enormous sum of £7,000 in five months of English concerts in 1823), Berlioz (in 1848, 1852 and 1855), Johann Strauss (The Father of the Waltz), Louis Spohr (who claimed to be the first conductor to use a baton, at a London concert in 1820) and many others also came.

Towards the end of the nineteenth century, native talent began to re-assert itself. William Sterndale Bennett was a noted composer and a friend of Mendelssohn and Schumann and Arthur Sullivan rose to fame and fortune with his operettas with Gilbert.

Three men, Sir Charles Villiers Stanford, Sir Hubert Parry and Sir Alexander Mackenzie, were responsible for what has been called 'the renaissance of English music' and opened the way for some of the greats of this century.

Two of the most outstanding Englishmen of the early twentieth century were Sir Edward Elgar and Frederick Delius, who died in 1934.

Elgar had a long and hard struggle for recognition. Many years of near poverty as a violinist and violin teacher preceded his first success at the age of forty-two with his *Enigma Variations* in 1899. A year later found him firmly established with his oratorio *Dream of Gerontius*, a work of almost Wagnerian power and style. He wrote two great symphonies, a violin concerto and a 'cello concerto, all very fine works; and it is ironical that most people know him best for his *Land of Hope and Glory*, merely a part of one of his five *Pomp and Circumstance* marches.

Frederick Delius, born in Bradford of German-Dutch descent, spent the first years of his adult life as an orange grower in Florida. The best known of his many works is *Brigg Fair*, written in a harmonic style of great charm and one which was Delius's own and has never been matched.

Ralph Vaughan Williams, as basically

Benjamin Britten (1913-19   )

Sir Edward Elgar (1857-1934)

The Royal Opera House, Covent Garden

English as his name, wrote nine symphonies, concertos for piano, violin and the tuba. He wrote his last symphony when he was eighty-five. His seventh symphony was based on the music he wrote for the film *Scott of the Antarctic*. Always willing to try anything new, he wrote a *Romance* for mouth organ and strings. Unlike so many people in *The Story of Music* Vaughan Williams was a late developer, only reaching his peak after the age of fifty.

Sir William Walton, born in 1902, was the first of the English modernists. His overture *Portsmouth Point* established a style of its own which was much copied. His *Belshazzar's Feast* was the most magnificent choral work since Elgar's *Gerontius* and easily the most popular. Walton's work includes violin, viola and 'cello concertos, an opera and several film scores of outstanding quality.

But probably no British composer born in this century can surpass Benjamin Britten,

Leader, founder and arch-practitioner of the English revolution in opera.

His first opera, *Peter Grimes*, opened with stunning effect in 1945, to be quickly followed by *The Rape of Lucretia* (1946), *Albert Herring* (1947), a new version of *The Beggar's Opera* (1948), *Let's Make an Opera* (1949), *Billy Budd* (1951), *Gloriana* (1953), *The Turn of the Screw* (1954), *Midsummer Night's Dream* (1954), *Noye's Fludde* (1958). One of his other works, *Variations and Fugue on a Theme of Purcell*, was written for a film 'The Young Person's Guide to the Orchestra'. His latest opera was given a TV première in 1971.

Britain today is a great centre of music, with five permanent symphony orchestras in London alone, Children's Concerts, Youth Orchestras, several ballet companies including the world famous Royal Opera House Ballet, the Sadler's Wells Opera Company, and many fine concert halls.

33 The New World

Very few Americans would recognise the following:

> *To Anacreon in heaven, as he sat in full glee*
> *A few sons of harmony made a petition*
> *That he their inspirer and patron would be,*
> *When this answer came down from that jolly*
> *old Grecian . . . .*

It comes from an eighteenth-century song called *Anacreon in Heaven*, written by John Stafford Smith, an Englishman of German extraction who was a choirboy and later organist at the Chapel Royal, London, in the late 1700s.

It was, in its day, a popular 'glee' – that is, an unaccompanied song for three or four male voices, usually sung at all-male get-togethers, a very popular pastime of the period, which later gave rise to the U.S. university Glee Clubs, although the latter usually have much wider musical range.

But there were Anacreontic Societies for the Singing of Glees (as they were called) in young America in the early eighteenth century as well as in Great Britain and they sang the same songs, including the one above, which was one of the most popular.

Thus when a young poet of Baltimore, Francis Scott Key, wrote the words for a stirring patriotic song, beginning:

> *Oh say, can you see by the dawn's early light*
> *What so proudly we hailed at the twilight's*
> *last gleaming*

he looked around for a song to fit his words (indeed, he may have had the song already in mind when he wrote the words, since the metre fits exactly), it was not too remarkable that he selected a song he had probably sung many times in his local Anacreontic Society. He threw out the old words (those which appear at the beginning of this chapter), replaced them with his own and called it *The Star Spangled Banner*.

The story goes that he was so eager to get his song into the hands of the public that it appeared on a handbill twenty-four hours after he had written it – that is, on 15 September 1814 – and he got it published in *The Baltimore Patriot* on the 20 September.

Famous as this song was to become throughout the world as the national anthem of the United States, it was not officially adopted as such until the Senate passed a Bill on 3 March 1931, ninety-seven years after it was written!

Music in the U.S. was inevitably much influenced by the kind of music which was played and sung in Great Britain at the time, whether that was of native origin or borrowed

from France, Germany or Italy. But by the 1800s German music dominated the concert halls of the U.S. and many of its brightest composers went to Germany to study.

One of the earliest of these venturesome pioneers was Edward MacDowell, who flourished at the end of the nineteenth century and who is still remembered for his romantic piano pieces.

By the early twentieth century, however, America's musical interest had swung to Paris and it was there that its musical sons (and daughters) went to study. Two of America's most famous and influential composers, Virgil Thomson and Aaron Copland, studied there under the gifted Frenchwoman, Nadia Boulanger, and were later to blend their American background with their European training— Thomson with revivalist hymn tunes, as in his 'cello concerto, and Copland with jazz and cowboy songs, as in the ballet *Appalachian Spring* and others.

Thomson, born in Kansas City in 1896, a graduate of Harvard and a winner of a Fellowship of the Julliard School of Music in 1923, has written symphonies and operas, notably *Four Saints in Three Acts*, film scores (*The River* and *Louisiana Story*), chamber music and many

other works, as well as being music critic of the *New York Herald Tribune* from 1940 to 1954.

Aaron Copland, born Aaron Kaplan in Brooklyn in 1900, also won a Fellowship, this time from the Guggenheim Foundation, in 1925. He has written much fine music – ballets, symphonies, piano music, film scores – *Billy the Kid, El Salon Mexico, Lincoln Portrait, Rodeo*, and the gentle *Quiet City* for woodwind, strings and brass – are some of his finest.

Two other pupils of Boulanger who were to become famous in their own right were Walter Piston and Roy Harris. The former was born in Maine in 1894, studied at Harvard and in Paris, and wrote a number of symphonies and other works as well as books on harmony, counterpoint and orchestration which are now standard works on these subjects.

Harris was another Guggenheim Fellowship holder, and was born in Oklahoma in 1898. Before going to Paris to study under Boulanger he was taught music by his mother. He has written many symphonies, choral works and much chamber music, and is a notable teacher.

One of Harris' teachers was Arthur Farwell, who was remarkable for having first studied engineering and suddenly gave it up to go to Germany and later to Paris, to take up music. Farwell's special contribution to American music is his wide and deep knowledge of American-Indian music of which he is the acknowledged master.

Charles Ives, born in Connecticut in 1874, combined a business career with brilliant composing talent, using techniques far in advance of his time, as did another gifted American composer, Roger Sessions.

Gian-Carlo Menotti, although of Italian birth, has lived most of his life in America, and has written many very successful operettas for the American stage and television which subsequently became world famous – *Amahl and the Night Visitors, The Telephone, The Medium, Amelia Goes to the Ball* and others.

One of the most striking native-born musicians was the greatest military band conductor and composer of all time, John Phillip Sousa, who was born in Washington, D.C. As well as having an outstanding gift for writing stirring marches (*Washington Post, Stars and Stripes for*

Leonard Bernstein (1918-19   )

Ever, El Capitan, and many more) he had a unique ability for drilling a military band into displays of musical viruosity that have never been equalled in their field. His line-up of a dozen trombones, playing all the way from a blasting fortissimo to a remarkably controlled pianissimo, his use of several piccolos playing florid obbligati of extreme technical difficulty against the melody, his invention of the 'sousaphone' – a base tuba with a huge flared bell turned forward over the player's head – and many other devices qualify him as a man of remarkable musical talents.

The special skill of American music is to absorb and use influences from all directions and turn them into specifically native forms. Not only the whole range of European classical music, but Latin-American, African, American-Indian and others, sung music or instrumental, find their expression in U.S. composition.

One of the most striking exponents of this was George Gershwin, born in Brooklyn. Originally a composer of popular songs, his talents led him into much wider fields and he startled the musical world of the 1920s with his *Rhapsody In Blue*, a work for full orchestra which is still much played today. This work, more than most, combined the talents of the symphony composer with the skills of the successful Tin Pan Alley song writer. (Tin Pan Alley is the legendary street in New York where live the publishers of the popular tunes of the moment, taking its name from the days of ragtime when 'tin pans' were part of the rhythmic stock-in-trade of the early ragtime drummers.) Gershwin went on to compose a piano concerto, orchestral music (*An American in Paris*), musical plays (*Of Thee I Sing*), a Negro folk opera (*Porgy and Bess*). He died in Hollywood at the early age of 39.

Leonard Bernstein (born in Lawrence, Massachusetts, 1918) is another gifted musician who has bridged the separate worlds of the symphony concert hall and the Broadway stage with mastery in both. A brilliant pianist, a conductor of world stature, he has written successful symphonies (*Jeremiah, The Age of Anxiety*), ballets (*Fancy Free*) as well as the enormously successful musicals *West Side Story, On the Town* and *Candide*.

Gershwin and Bernstein are outstanding examples of the American gift for combining local background with music.

Jazz, as the only truly alive folk music of the twentieth century, is a prime example of this and is dealt with in the next chapter. But another field in which American music is pre-eminent is the musical play, direct descendant of European opera and operetta, exemplified by *Oklahoma, Showboat, Sound of Music*, and many others, in which the music and dancing reach a remarkably high level.

The American symphony orchestras rank among the most technically proficient in the world and, under native-born as well as imported conductors, provide centres of music of which any country could well be proud.

Part of this American awareness of music is reflected in the level of the musical colleges and conservatories, where modern forms of music are given as much attention as the older, and where internationally famous musicians such as Piston, Milhaud, Hindemith and others are appointed to high positions. The opportunities for young people to learn music in all its forms are probably wider in America than in any other country.

As this chapter opened with the story of the origin of *The Star Spangled Banner*, it may be appropriate to finish it with the story of the origin of that other great American anthem, *America*, or *My Country 'Tis of Thee*, the tune of which is exactly the same as that of the British national anthem, *God Save the Queen*, a fact which frequently causes surprise to Americans visiting England for the first time and to Britons visiting America.

Nobody knows who wrote the tune of *God Save the Queen*, although the name of John Bull, a sixteenth century organist, is frequently used in this context because a version of the tune in the minor appears in one of his keyboard pieces. It would seem to be much earlier than this although its widespread use did not occur until about 1745 when Prince Charles, the Young Pretender, landed in Scotland in an attempt to seize the throne, and the people in the theatres sang the tune to show their support.

The tune has been borrowed by some twenty nations as their national song and in America it has been set to many different words – *God Save America, God Save George Washington, God Save the Thirteen States* and so on, culminating in *My Country 'Tis of Thee*, written in 1831 by the Rev. Samuel Francis Smith.

Many composers, Weber, Brahms, and Beethoven among them, have used the tune in their works, and the prime phrase, 'God Save the King', goes back as far as the Old Testament in connection with Saul, Absalom and Jehoash.

Louis Armstrong

34 The Jazz Scene

Perhaps the most interesting side development of music in the twentieth century is jazz. There has never been anything else quite like it.

There have been many other side developments of music like gipsy music, brass band music, accordion music, lute music – but nothing with the all-enveloping attraction and drive of jazz.

Nor has any subsection of music ever had so much written about it; critically, historically and explanatorily. Yet despite all this, it defies analysis. It is in part music for dancing, but it is more than that; it is the popular music of the people, but lots of people do not like it; it has a steady unbroken rhythm, but so do marches; it co-exists with popular songs of the moment, but much of it has no words.

Nobody seems to know for certain where it got its name. There have been many theories, none of them very convincing. The most likely seems to be that it is a distortion of a forgotten Negro slang phrase: to 'jass' something, meaning to play with it, alter it, mess it up.

Its origin as a music form, however, is a little clearer. It almost certainly began when the coloured slaves were brought from Africa to work in the cotton plantations of the United States. Bringing with them the strong sense of rhythm possessed by all primitive peoples, they added it to the traditional songs and hymns of their white owners.

Firstly, no doubt, their early songs were sad and dirgeful as they had little to be happy about. From these grew the bitter-sweet songs and tunes that we know as 'blues'; derived from the use of the word 'blue' to mean depressed or unhappy. There is a traceable history of blues singing as far back as 1860 and almost certainly it was in existence long before that. In later years the blues developed a fixed pattern of a 12-bar tune with the flattened 3rd and 7th notes of the scale predominating in the harmony.

There must also have been happy occasions when the music brightened up – became faster, even more heavily rhythmic and when sheer exuberance and high spirits took over and added embellishment and variation to the tunes. Here, almost certainly, was the birth of jazz.

Later, they began to learn instruments by ear and to play the same tunes and variations that they had previously sung. The addition of drums, either actual orchestral instruments or just anything that responded when beaten, would powerfully reinforce the instinctive rhythm that was already present in the performers' playing and singing.

Groups of players began to get together. Jazz bands were used by the coloured people in New Orleans and other Southern towns for dances and marches as well as for funerals; slow and

bluesy when going to the funeral, bright and rhythmic when coming back.

Jazz, although still rough and uncultured, began to develop its own idiom and style unlike anything else in music.

Towards the end of the last century another and parallel form of music began to come forward – ragtime. Just how much ragtime derived from jazz is impossible to say. Certainly it had many similarities; the small group of instruments (usually piano, drums, banjo, trumpet or trombone, saxophone or clarinet), the wild extemporisations (making it up as they went along), the fixed rhythm and tempo (steady speed). And yet there was a difference, possibly derived from the fact that most of the players of ragtime were white rather than black. The all-white Dixieland Jazz Band became world

famous in 1915 and started a craze that persisted in Europe and America late into the 1920s.

By then it was attracting the attention of more serious musicians. Debussy wrote *Golli-wog's Cake-Walk* in 1908; Stravinsky wrote *Piano Rag-Music* and *Ragtime*. Ravel, Hindemith, Mailhaud, Constant Lambert and others also also tried their hands at the idiom but their academic training got in the way and their attempts were never anything but a poor imitation of the real thing.

Ragtime eventually died and jazz reigned undisputed in its place. Then came the era of 'swing', which was an attempt to take the improvisatory character of jazz and harness it to big bands and orchestrations. Benny Goodman, Count Basie, Duke Ellington, Glen Miller and others were the big band stars of the 1930s

ABOVE: *Louis Armstrong playing in a jam session*

BELOW: *Duke Ellington*

Jazz of the popular radio and TV programmes

and 40s, with virtuoso instrumental soloists like Louis Armstrong, Joe Venuti, Django Rhinehart, Coleman Hawkins and many others utilising their undoubted talents playing with small groups, mostly for recording, and creating a very large number of gramophone records still much prized by collectors all over the world.

Today the big band is almost extinct, killed off partly by changing tastes in entertainment, partly by the costliness of maintaining such organisations. The small group and the soloist are very much alive and such units as the Modern Jazz Quartette, Charlie Parker, Ornette Coleman and others have advanced so far from their musical forbears that their music is hardly recognisable as coming from the same source.

Advanced modern jazz is today an intellectual music, written and performed by conservatory-trained musicians, and having much in common with the more advanced forms of chamber music.

This, of course, is not the jazz of the popular radio and television programmes, which is an altogether simpler form, far closer to its robust forbears.

The Who

35 Pop – Music of Youth

Jazz, as described in the previous chapter, is getting on for a hundred years old. It has grown up and through the plantation beginnings, ragtime, swing, big band, and arrived at two separate styles – the way out advanced kind and the popular every day sort.

The former has a relatively small though intensely interested and devoted following. The latter is the sort of music that accompanies popular entertainment – the devotees of the former style refuse to accept that the latter is jazz at all.

What then has filled the vast gap left? The answer is, as everyone knows, 'pop'.

This short and explosive monosyllable (deriving, one supposes, from the term 'popular music') is without any doubt the music most liked by the enormous majority of young people of today, anywhere in the world.

Where did pop come from? That is fairly easy to answer – it is the obvious descendant and derivative of middle-of-the-road jazz, the preferred music of the young people of the previous generation. But, though it may be a descendant, it is certainly very different. It is not a matter of subtle alteration in fashion or style; there are such deep differences that the admirer of jazz will not be found dead with pop, and the pop addict tends to think of jazz as insufferably square. Yet the two kinds of music have common parentage. Where lies the difference?

The breakaway from the line of ordinary jazz almost certainly started with the invention of the electric guitar in the early 1950s. Before this, guitars had been electrically amplified not

Rod Stewart of The Small Faces   RIGHT: *Jimi Hendrix*

only for recording and broadcasting but for large-hall playing where the instrument would have been inaudible without amplification. But these were ordinary acoustic guitars (the traditional hollow-bodied wooden type) with microphones placed either near them or actually attached. Then it occurred to some inventive genius that if the sound were to be always microphonically amplified there was no need for the hollow box-like body – why not amplify the strings direct?

This produced a totally new sound. More than that, it produced a new *range* of sounds, with vibrators and the like, that had never been heard before. It also produced a volume that could dominate everything else around with the mere turn of a knob.

Couple these features with the fact that if you limit your requirements to a handful of chords, and make life even easier by using a 'capo' (a movable handcuff-like device fastened to the neck of the guitar) to avoid the necessity of requiring a fresh set of chord shapes for

each change of key, then the six-string guitar becomes a fairly easy instrument to play.

This new sound and the ease with which it was produced undoubtedly had a very great deal to do with producing a new race of performers with new ideas about singing and accompaniment. The time was ripe for something new.

It is impossible to say who were the first pop singers or groups. New and powerful ideas like this do not spring into being overnight, complete and developed. Someone tries a small new idea; someone else borrows and adapts it; someone else takes the adaption and adds yet another idea; and so on. Performers begin to emerge and to catch the public's attention; not because they invented the style but because they happen to do it better than the next.

'Skiffle' was probably the first real new style. It featured electric guitars, 'washboards' and a faked-up string bass. And the young people liked its driving sound. Skiffle groups flowered, spread until they became ten-a-penny,

106

then withered in the face of the more sophisticated 'rock 'n' roll', which used the same vitally important electric guitars but abandoned the gimmickry of the washboards and the one-string bass.

Since then the instrumentation has varied very little. A bass guitar, using four longer and heavier strings, was introduced and this provided a good 'bottom' and harmonic foundation for the other guitars – usually two in number, one 'lead' and one 'accompaniment' or 'rhythm'. To this basic rock 'n' roll formation was added any instruments which took the organiser's fancy (piano, drums, bass, trumpet, saxophone et cetera). Mostly this settled down to the now standard three guitars and drums.

This was a compact unit, capable of tremendous drive and rhythm, not demanding much in the way of instrumental technique (although there were some extremely good players among the groups), and needing little or nothing in the way of written orchestrations, which was just as well, since many of these new performers had limited ability when it came to reading music.

But with such small numbers it was possible to work out ingenious changes and effects and learn them off by heart. And all members sang, either with the others or alone. The quality of the voice did not matter as great deal, so long as the singer had the right style.

The fabulous Beatles were the undisputed masters of this kind of music and they had exceptional talent when it came to writing songs in the new genre.

Since their retirement there has been endless claimants to the title of 'the greatest'. The Rolling Stones probably came closest to inheriting their crown, although their music was completely different in style.

The Who, Credence Clearwater, The Small Faces, Led Zeppelin and scores more have their followings. The bizarre names they give themselves, and their almost uniform clothes and hair styles, are all part of the image.

And, as with all art forms, there are some performers who prefer to explore the unusual and untried, producing music which is unlike anything else, even in its own genre. Such groups as the Soft Machine, with its weird harmonies and far out rhythms, are as far from

Credence Clearwater

the Beatles as the Modern Jazz Quartette is from the Dixieland Jazz Band, or as Stravinsky is from Haydn.

One of the more remarkable aspects of pop is the outstanding success of certain solo singers. Whether they are properly described as pop singers, or folk singers, or rhythm-and-blues singers, matters not a great deal. They are an essential part of the pop scene and have to be considered with it.

Elvis Presley was the first super star of the rock era. With scores of LPs and singles behind him, plus a number of films, his appeal seems almost indestructible. The Mississippi-born singer was discovered at the age of nineteen in the middle 50s when he went into a recording studio to make a private recording for his mother's birthday. The head of the studio in Memphis spotted a special talent and Presley was on his way to the star position he has held ever since.

Another remarkable singer of a totally different type is Bob Dylan. Many say that he is the most remarkable of them all. Dylan's contribution to the pop scene was not his singing or his guitar playing, but his lyrics.

At the beginning of his career he was labelled as a 'protest singer'. He wrote and sang about such subjects as the futility of war and struck an immediate response from those of his own generation who wanted someone to express their ideas and present them in a style of music that was their very own. Naive as much of the philosophizing was, it was expressed in a quality of writing far above that of the average pop lyric. Songs like *Desolation Row, God On Our Side, Times They Are A-Changing* are a long way advanced from the 'June-moon' type of earlier popular songs. There is no doubt that Dylan has a considerable and far reaching effect on the music of his generation.

It is not possible to do more than mention the names of the thousands of singers and players who have contributed something to this musical genre. Some were gifted superstar performers, like Frank Sinatra and Judy Garland; some were vital and driving personalities, like Chubby Checker, Jimi Hendrix and Bill Haley (whose *Rock Around The Clock* was a riot-causing landmark in the early days of pop); some were smoothly polished stage and television performers like Cliff Richard and Tom Jones. But all, in their various ways, influenced or were influenced by pop.

The Beatles, already mentioned, had an exceptional flair for melody, harmonic invention and unusual lyrics. They were also polished showmen and indefatigable spreaders of the pop culture. It is probable that they did more than anybody else to establish a focal point for the young people of all countries. Everywhere in the world, including Soviet Russia, has felt their influence, whether it was in their hair styles or their music or both.

It was inevitable, of course, that such a vigorous form of popular music would be derided by the more conservative minded – every generation prefers its own music. It was equally inevitable that pop would be taken up by the cultists and extended into fields where it never expected to find itself.

There have been many attempts to combine pop music with concert hall music, as for example in John Lord's *Concerto for Group and Orchestra*, written for the Deep Purple group and performed in conjunction with the Royal Philharmonic Orchestra, but the combination of the two kinds of music has not been very successful.

A more promising approach has been the rock operas such as *Jesus Christ Superstar, Godspell* and others; where the music, although given a far wider importance than previously, nevertheless has kept firmly to its own style.

Led Zeppelin

36 Electronic Sounds

Electronic music is in a class of its own. It uses none of the known orchestral instruments and mostly defies ordinary notation. Its sounds can range from the gentle and soothing to the jarring and shrieking. It is an acquired taste but its admirers are as sincere in their appreciation as any other section of music lovers.

It is essential not to confuse electronic music with electronically amplified ordinary music, which uses standard orchestral instruments and merely makes them louder by the use of microphones. Electronic music, or electrophonic music as some prefer to call it, is basically produced by causing radio valves (or transistors) to 'heterodyne' or 'whistle' – a controlled version of the noise made by an ill-tuned radio set.

Another way of producing the sound is by rotating discs in front of a photo-electric cell.

There is an almost endless variety of names for the instruments; the Theremin, Dynaphone, Rhythmicon, Photona and so on, according to the whim of the inventor. The method of playing them varies almost as widely. One of the earliest, the Theremin, was played by moving the hands about in the air at different distances from a single metal rod which protruded from the instrument. Later instruments have a piano keyboard and masses of switches and resistances.

Electronic recording tape is also used in some of these instruments, recorded sounds being manipulated and altered to produce completely new sounds.

Some of these instruments are built to produce the standard notes, although of a very different quality from anything else; some are built to produce quarter-tones or less; some have infinite variation at the control of the performer.

There are two completely different ways of producing the sounds of electronic music. One is to generate a single uncomplicated 'sine tone' – a simple, bare sound, and then add other sounds until a satisfactory effect is produced. The other way is to produce what is called 'white sound'; being a solid wall of noise which contains every possible frequency, and then to filter out what is not required.

Electronic music, therefore, can consist either of these manufactured sounds or, in more modern instruments, the finished sound originated directly from the instrument. The most advanced of these instruments is the Moog synthesiser, an extremely complex and costly instrument, with banks of dials and switches and a piano keyboard.

Much experimental composing has been done with electronic music. Some of the work has been worked out mathematically to produce the required tones. Other works have been based on the connection and compilation of sounds produced at random. Stockhausen, Eimert and Křenek are some of the distinguished composers who have explored this field.

A totally different, though related, form of music is 'musique concrète'. This is music built up from tape recordings of ordinary sounds – like a bell ringing, a door slamming, a factory whistle. These sounds are then manipulated on tape – it could be, for instance, played backwards, or the actual door slam deleted and only the reverberation left. Some quite remarkable effects have been obtained and whole compositions made from endless manipulations of one simple sound such as water splashing into a bowl. The American John Cage is a leading exponent of this kind of music but is also famous for his composition *Imaginary Landscapes for Twelve Radios*, which is scored for 'radio frequencies and volumes resulting in chance sounds'.

The Moog Synthesiser is one of the most advanced electronic instruments

37 Into the Future

Nobody can tell with any certainty what the future has in store. Did the monks of the fifth century, as they sang their simple one-line plainsongs, ever imagine the complexity and majesty of a massed orchestra and choir performance of Handel's *Messiah*? Did the wandering groups of minstrel lute players of medieval times foresee the Beatles? Did Beethoven, battling against the social prejudice of his times when musicians were household servants of lesser standing than cooks, ever think they could receive titles of nobility and have their own mansions and castles and servants?

Above all, did any of them foresee the tape recorder, the Moog synthesizer, radio, television?

And if they did not – and it is almost certain that they did not – how can we make any reasonable guesses about the future?

Well, we can – provided we proceed very cautiously.

For instance, it seems highly unlikely that the great stirring music of the past will ever be entirely discarded and forgotten. As long as man remains a civilised creature, and has ears and emotions to be reached through them, then surely that magic something which great music has, will remain potent. In short, Forecast Number One is that the great music of the past will still be played into the far future. How it will be played; whether by humans or machines, is a different matter. But it will be played.

By machines? This is possible at the moment if we mean only instruments of reproduction. Records, tapes, cassettes, hi-fi – these are commonplaces which, nevertheless, would have astounded our forefathers. These will continue, with ever increasing purity of sound and convenience of reproduction. It is not inconceivable for instance, that in the future a

The newly completed Opera House in Sydney, Australia, designed to resemble a ship in full sail

musical item for the length of a symphony or an opera or a pop festival will be stored in something no bigger than a pin's head or a length of hair-thin wire.

But these would still be reproducing devices. What about making the music – either originating the composition or playing someone else's? Composition by computer is already here, and deadly dull it is, lacking totally that inspiration that marks the difference between any old music and great music. As long as mankind remains a creative individual he will go on making music out of the mystery that is musical imagination. So – reproduction? Yes. Creativity? No.

What about playing? Many people get intense pleasure from playing an instrument for their own satisfaction. They like producing a medley of sounds by scraping, blowing,

112

tapping or pressing. This, is therefore, most unlikely to disappear although the instruments themselves and the methods of operating them will undoubtedly change. However, there is an urgent need for a genius who can take the drudgery out of practice! And who knows? In the future, it may be possible to have skill with a musical instrument added instantly by hypnotism, or grafted on by plastic surgery.

What about new music? There is no doubt whatever that that will change. It has been changing for thousands of years and there is no reason why it should cease doing so. And it will not sound much like anything we know now.

The adjustment of the human ear to new sounds is a slow process. Wagner's harmonies shocked the musical world but today they are considered commonplace. But it took over a hundred hears.

Schönberg, Berg and Webern music is equally unacceptable to most modern ears – but that appeared less than fifty years ago. Today, the experimenters with musical sounds make noises that all but a handful of devotees find excruciatingly awful – 'Not only just noise', they say, 'but horrible noise'. Almost exactly the same words as those used by Nicholas Rubenstein when he refused to play the piano work which Tchaikovsky had dedicated to him in the mistaken belief that Rubenstein would appreciate new ideas; or even those used about the sixth century Roman scholar Cassiodorus, when he suggested it might be a good idea to sing two different notes simultaneously.

Forecast Number Two, therefore, is that the music of the future will not sound even remotely like the music of today. And if we could hear it now, we would probably hate it.

38 Reading a Score

A 'score' is a written or printed piece of music with all the parts for the separate instruments (or voices) set down one below the other. It has three uses; (a) composers of orchestral works think in terms of a complete orchestral sound – they hear in their heads (just as the deaf Beethoven did) the combined effect of all the instruments playing together. The score is the way of writing down this combined sound as they conceive it; (b) it is the information book which the conductor uses to rehearse and guide the orchestra; and (c) it is the method by which an orchestrator or arranger turns a simple one-line tune into a work for an orchestra of several dozen instruments. It has other uses; for instance, it is a neat and simple way of storing the composer's thoughts for future use; many people like to read scores as one would a book, or to take one with them to a concert and follow with their eyes as well as with their ears what is going on.

In compiling a score the writer must think what kind of mood he wishes to express – happy, sad, menacing, soothing, exciting, or whatever – and then decide how he is going to convey this musically. This is the inspirational part. Next his technical knowledge of instruments comes into play, how they sound separately and in an infinite variety of combinations; he must know the range, sound, capabilities and limitations of every instrument in the orchestra.

He must also know harmony very thoroughly indeed – what combinations of notes go together, how to change key (modulate) and how to use all the devices of counterpoint, fugue, canon, and many more technical points.

Finally, he has to learn to write in several different keys at once for the benefit of transposing instruments (those which, in order to facilitate fingering or for other reasons are built in a pitch or key different from that of the other instruments).

Here is a single page of score for full orchestra. Although it may look a lot it is in fact only four bars of a composition that might contain many hundreds, if not thousands, of bars. Unlike the music for a single instrument, or the lines in a book, you do not read the top line, then the second, then the third and so on. You read all the lines at once – that is why the whole page consists only of four bars and would last, say, only seven or eight seconds.

As you will see, the instruments are set out in groups, one below the other, in order of pitch. At the top are the wood wind (piccolo, two flutes, two oboes, cor anglais, two clarinets, bass clarinet, two bassoons, contra bassoon – note that the cor anglais and clarinets are in different keys from the rest, since they are 'transposing' instruments).

Then comes the brass (four horns, three trumpets, two trombones, bass (III) trombone and tuba – the horns and trumpets being transposing). You will note that some of the instruments are in the treble clef some in the bass clef – this is in order to keep their parts more or less within the stave to avoid having lots of 'leger' lines (lines above or below the stave).

Next comes the percussion (note the curious shape of the notes for the cymbal, meaning it has duration but no pitch), and the timpani, which have different notes and a key signature – the wavy line over the top meaning a 'roll'.

Then the harp and piano – the former with the first eight notes of a 23-note glissando written out in full to show what sharps or flats are required, and the remainder indicated by a wavy line.

Finally the strings – 1st (A) and 2nd (B) violins (there may be dozens of each of these but they would all play the same notes); viola (ditto and note the special 'alto' clef, midway between treble and bass); 'cello (ditto); and string bass.

All this for just a few seconds of playing time! Just imagine the effort that went into a Beethoven symphony lasting the best part of an hour, or into Mahler's *Symphony of a Thousand*, which called for 130 players; eight vocal soloists, two full choirs and a third choir of 400 children!

THE STORY OF MUSIC

Nicholas Ingman

39 The Language of Music

The Introduction said that this is not a textbook and therefore it will not include a Glossary of Musical Terms.

Nevertheless, music does have many words and phrases which do not occur in ordinary everyday language, and no matter how much one might want to remain untechnical, an understanding of the principal ones is essential unless one is constantly to trip over unknown words.

Most of these words are borrowings from Italian, French or German – for the obvious reason that since so many great musicians were of those nationalities, their native words inevitably crept into general musical usage.

One cannot read a concert program without encountering such phrases as 'The *andante cantabile* in the first movement . . .' This leaves the untrained person mystified and a little irritated. There is no need, since all it means is 'The slowish bit written in a singable style . . .

So here is a list of words and phrases which are likely to be met in reading other books about music, lives of the great men, or even newspaper reports.

A Capella (or just Capella): Originally meant 'In the church, or chapel, style'. Now means unaccompanied singing.

Accelerando: Getting quicker.

Adagio: Slow – a slow movement.

Adeste Fideles: The name of a very famous hymn dating from the early eighteenth century ('O come, All Ye Faithful').

Ad lib or *Ad libitum:* 'At will' – meaning playing or singing the passage so marked in your own style or speed. Sometimes refers to a passage that can be included or left out as desired.

Agitato: In an agitated manner. Usually fast music to indicate or accompany something exciting, like a cowboy chase, or a battle scene.

Air: Melody, tune.

Alla Breve: Time signature, meaning 'take half a breve as the time beat'.

Allegretto: Bright and lively.

Allegro: Even more bright and lively.

Alto: High, applied to voices and instruments – e.g. alto in the choir, alto saxophone.

Amore: Love. *Con amore* – with loving feeling.

Andante: Slowish but not slow.

Antiphon: Short verse of a psalm sung alternately by two choirs.

Aria: A long and well-developed solo vocal piece.

Arrangement: Adaptation of a musical piece. In modern usage means 'orchestration' (which see).

Ballad: Originally a song to be danced to but now means a simple story-telling song.

Band: Musical group of wind and percussion but not containing strings.

Bar: A short division of music, contained between one bar line and the next. (American equivalent = measure.)

Bass: Lowest voice or instrument or part of the harmony.

Blues: Bitter-sweet slow jazz song of twelve bars.

Brass: Instruments played with a cup mouthpiece, such as cornet, trumpet, trombone, tuba etc., sometimes made of other metals but still described as 'brass'.

Brass band: Group made up of brass instruments and percussion.

Cadence or *Close:* End of a composition or phrase.

Cadenza: Florid ad lib solo passage for instrument or voice.

Canon: Passages of music in which one strand or voice imitates, or echoes, another. For example, *Sumer is I-cumen In.*

Cantata: Work for several solo voices and chorus, like a short oratorio, or opera without scenery or acting. Usually, but not necessarily, on a religious theme.

Catch: Short round (vocal canon) in medieval popular song style.

Chamber Music: Music for small group of instruments, each instrument being on equal terms with the others.

Choral or *Chorale:* Hymn tunes sung by small

groups of singers or whole congregations.

Chromatic: Every note in the scale, including sharps and flats.

Classical Music: Music of permanent value.

Coda: Tail; end piece.

Coloratura: Singing decorated with runs, cadenzas and other showy devices.

Concerto: Difficult work for solo instrument and orchestra, but can be written for several instruments or even for orchestra only.

Counterpoint: Combination of several voices or parts, often in imitation, the parts moving horizontally.

Crotchet: Black note with single tail. (American = quarter note).

Diatonic: Notes of a given scale or key, as distinct from chromatic (which see).

Duet: Combination by or for two performers.

Dynamics: Variations in strength, accent etc.

Etude: A study, or short piece intended as a method of self improvement for the performer but raised by Chopin into an art in itself.

Fiddle: Slang name for any bowed instrument but particularly the violin.

Flat: Sign placed before a note to lower it a semitone. Also inadvertently playing or singing below the proper pitch. (Opposite = 'sharp'.)

Form: The changing and developing of musical ideas to avoid the two extremes of monotonous repetition and constant difference. The 'shape' of musical compositions. For example, 'ternary form' means a work in which the first section is complete in itself, the second section a contrast in material and key, and the third the first one repeated.

Fugue: A complicated form in which the interweaving of themes and counter-themes, the alternation of keys and so on, are worked out in an elaborate and complicated manner.

Glee: Short, unaccompanied piece for male voices in block harmony (i.e., not contrapuntal).

Harmonics: Secondary parts of a basic note (also called overtones or upper partials). In stringed instruments produced by lightly touching strings rather than pressing them down firmly.

Harmonica: American name for mouth organ. Originally musical glasses activated by touching or rubbing, performed on by Mozart as a boy, and written for by Beethoven and others.

Harmony: 'The clothing of melody' or the addition of other supporting and blending notes. Began in the ninth century. Not used in Eastern music.

Intonation: Singing or playing 'in tune' – i.e., neither flat nor sharp.

Jam Session: Jazz musicians improvising together.

Key: The material of any particular scale. The number of sharps and flats in a 'key signature'. Came into use in the early seventeenth century.

Klavier or *Clavier:* German name for any keyboard instrument – harpsichord, clavichord, pianoforte.

Largo: Very slow and broad.

Leitmotiv or *Leading Motive:* Theme used to represent characters or situations and constantly repeated to signify them.

Lieder: Distinctive type of song in which the poetic words are of first importance. Schubert wrote over 600 lieder.

Madrigal: Unaccompanied songs for 2, 3 or 4 voices with ingenious counterpoint. Originally thirteenth century Italian, became very popular in England in late sixteenth century.

Masque: Musical entertainment, originally Italian, but much practised in England in the sixteenth century. Included poetry, singing, dancing, mime, acting, costume and scenery – all applied to the representation of allegorical subjects.

Mass: Musical setting of the Roman Catholic religious ceremony.

Measure: See Bar.

Melody: Tune; one line of notes, unsupported by harmony.

Metronome: Mechanical device for fixing the tempo of a composition by giving out a loud tick, which can be set at various speeds. Composers sometimes give their works metronome markings to indicate speeds at which they are to be played.

Motet: Religious pieces for several voices, with parts moving at different lengths of notes. Introduced into the Roman Catholic service. Palestrina wrote 180 of them.

Motif: A phrase of anything beyond two notes

which is capable of standing on its own and also of being developed into a longer passage.

Neumes: Sings placed over words to remind singers of the tune. Used before notation was invented.

Oratorio: Major religious work for solo vocalists, chorus and orchestra for either concert or church performance.

Orchestration: The writing of parts for the instruments of the orchestra from single-line melody or other source.

Programme Music: Instrumental music that attempts to evoke literary ideas or mental pictures. The opposite is Absolute, or Abstract, Music.

Recitative: Type of vocal music which is more spoken than sung.

Rallentando, Ritenuto: Slowing down, holding back.

Score: Written or printed music which shows the whole of the music for all instruments or voices, as distinct from the separate parts.

Sonata: An instrumental composition (as distinct from Cantata = sung composition) usually in four distinct movements, basically for piano solo or violin and piano, but often extended to trios, quartetes etc.

Staff or *Stave:* The five lines on which music is written.

Symphony: Sonata for full orchestra. Major work in four or more movements.

Temperament: Adjustment in tuning whereby paired notes such B-sharp and C, or D-flat and C-sharp, are played by one key instead of two, a compromise which leaves neither note completely accurate but near enough for the ear to accept them.

Transposing, Transposition: Altering the whole of a piece to a different key (i.e., pitch) without in any way changing the tune. Certain instruments (e.g. trumpet, saxophone) always play at transposed pitch in order to simplify fingering, the orchestrator making due allowance for this when writing the score.

Virtuoso: Instrumentalist of exceptional skill.

Voluntary: Any extemporary performance on any instrument, but used mostly for organists. Voluntaries can also be written – e.g., Jeremiah Clarke's *Trumpet Voluntary.*

Wood Wind: Group of instruments, originally made from wood but now made just as often from metal, in which the sound is created by reeds (clarinet, oboe, bassoon, saxophone) or by blowing across open holes (flute, recorder).

40 Instruments of the Orchestra

1 Prehistoric

The very first 'instruments' were probably the human hands – clapping them together, or slapping the body, the arms, the armpits, the thighs.

This 'slapping music' exists to this very day, a million years later, among certain primitive tribes, even in children's games ('Clap hands!'), and in the Swiss schuhplattertanz, in which the dancers slap their leather shorts, their shoes, their bodies and even each other's faces!

At that distant period, too, the voice could be included as an 'instrument', and perhaps whistling to imitate the wind.

Before very long, however, primitive man must have discovered that he could improve on

Two prehistoric bone whistles

these personal' instruments by beating or hitting something else – a tree trunk, an animal bone, a stone – two stones together, a piece of animal skin.

None of these would produce 'music' or even musical notes, but they would produce rhythms and different sounds, and that is probably as far as primitive man was able to go.

But it would not stay like that. Accident or design would reveal that even more attractive sounds could be produced if one did something to those bits of wood and bone.

For instance, the tree trunk made a better sound if it was hollowed out and a slit cut in it (slit drums just like this are still in use today among savage tribes in the jungle). Or rubbing a piece of bone against another piece, especially if one had a sharp edge. Stamping the feet, too, over a covered hole in the ground would make an agreeable booming noise.

After a while these simple sounds would develop into quite a collection of 'instruments', some of which have been dug up thousands of years later.

Rattles, made of hollowed stone; scrapers made of a split bone which would make a rhythmic noise when scraped against a piece of tree; shakers made of teeth or perhaps a large fruit shell with nuts or small stones inside (like a baby's rattle of today). And something quite remarkable – a piece of flat bone or shaped wood with a hole at one end, through which was threaded a string, the device being whirled round the head to produce a whirring, roaring sound that must have been quite exciting. We know about this partly because such relics have been dug up and partly because some primitive tribes in Australia still use them. They are called bull roarers.

Most important of all, however, would be a hollow bone which produced a humming or whistling noise when blown across the top (like blowing into a bottle). This was important because it was the remote forerunner of all wind instruments – the clarinet, the flute, even the trumpet and trombone – all of which operate on exactly the same principle of producing a sound by agitating a column of air enclosed in a tube.

All this occured something like 500,000

119

COMPOSITION OF
A SYMPHONY ORCHESTRA

The size of a symphony orchestra varies considerably according to the works to be played, the wishes of the conductor and the resources available. Thus there may be anything from 60 to 120 players, with an average of about 87, as in this picture of one of the BBC Symphony Orchestras.

Variations in size occur mostly in the string section, where numbers are increased mostly to improve volume and balance rather than to add to the harmonic richness.

Less usual instruments such as the celesta, saxophone, bass clarinet et cetera, are added if the composer's score calls for them. The piano is very seldom included except as a solo instrument.

The way in which the groups of instruments are set out varies according to the wishes of the conductor or the size and shape of the stage. The one shown is typical of most.

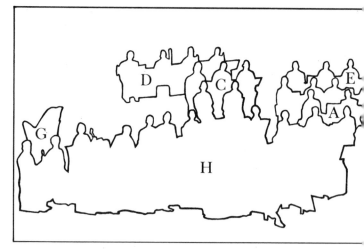

WOODWIND SECTION

A   Flutes (also playing piccolos)/2
      Oboes/2   Cor Anglais/1

B   Clarinets (one playing bass clarinet)/3
      Bassoons/2   Contra bassoon/1

BRASS SECTION

C   Trumpets/3

D   Trombones/2   Bass trombone/1   Tuba/1

E   French horns/5

PERCUSSION

F   Timpani/1   Snare drum/1
      Bass drum & cymbals/1
      Glockenspiel & xylophone/1

HARP

G   Harp/1

STRING SECTION

H   Violins (1st and 2nd)/29

J   Violas/12

K   'Cellos/10

L   Double basses/8

TOTAL/87 (plus conductor)

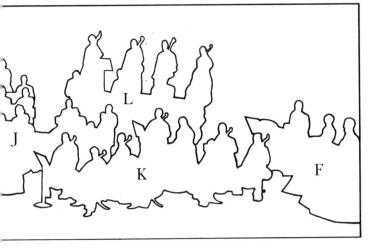

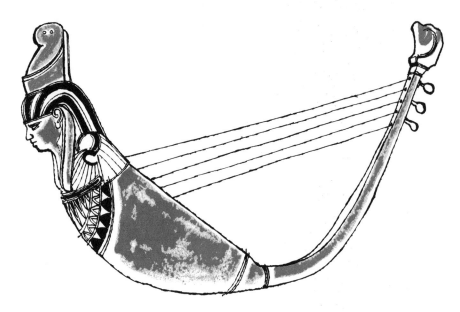

An Egyptian harp

years ago, in what are called Paleolithic (Stone Age) times, and already we had two groups or classifications of instruments–percussion (those that are struck) and wind-blown.

Passing on a few hundred thousand years to Neolithic (New Stone Age) times, we find our primitive musician has not only improved what instruments he had but added a few more.

The bone whistle now has a hole, or even more than one hole, pierced in the side, enabling more than one note to be obtained from the same piece of tubing (just like a modern flute, or recorder, or oboe). This was a tremendous stride forward, because it indicated a consciousness of pitch–of the attraction of different notes played one after the other. (Bone whistles with holes, 25,000 years old, have been found.)

Man had also discovered that if you made a noise into a shell it was magnified (like the modern megaphone) and, even more important, that if he pursed his lips and blew into a hole in the pointed end (that is, made an embouchure, as modern brass instrument players call it) a note was sounded. This was the birth of all the brass instruments, like cornets and trumpets and trombones.

And he made his first primitive xylophone – bits of wood, or stone, of different sizes which gave out notes of different pitch when struck.

Finally, from 10,000–20,000 years ago have been found fragments of drums–real drums with holes round the edge that suggest skin was stretched over the end.

Thus, therefore, we can say that long before man was 'civilised' he had discovered, or invented, all the basic instruments – the flute, the trumpet, the plucked string, the drum. Tens of thousands of years were to pass, of course, and many thousands of variations were to be gone through, before the modern orchestral instruments of exquisite tone and manufacture were to be arrived at – but the *principles* had been discovered and put to use.

2 Early Civilisations

By the time of the early civilisations of the Sumerians, the Babylonians, the Assyrians and the Egyptians, the primitive instruments had been much developed and improved.

The shell trumpet, for instance, had become a ram's horn and, as soon as bronze making became established, a metal tube. The change from animal horn to metal tube was important, because it removed the natural limitations of size and shape.

Bronze instruments called lurs, three or four feet long, with a mouthpiece and a flared bell, have been dug up in Sweden and dated at several thousand years ago.

Sumer, Babylonia and the adjacent countries developed the bowman's plucked string into the harp. First, no doubt, it had a single string

122

The hydraulus, early water organ, dating from 250 BC

A bull-roarer

stretched from some kind of sound box, which might have been a tortoise's shell, to a neck of some kind. Then other strings would be added, perhaps at different tensions to give different notes, or perhaps of different length, which would also give different notes.

Thus was born the harp and the lyre. The difference is that a *harp* consisted of an angle or curve of wood with the strings stretched in ever-decreasing lengths, from one end to the other. The lower end would be a box of some kind to magnify the weak noise of the plucked string. The *lyre* consisted of *two* uprights attached to the soundbox, with a cross piece at the top from which the strings were fixed to the sound box.

The harp and the lyre are first cousins, and what makes them so is that the strings are always 'open' – that is, not artifically shortened by being 'stopped' by pressure of the fingers. Both instruments are played by plucking individual strings, or by 'sweeping' all the strings, as does the modern orchestral harpist.

The *lute* is entirely different in principal. The string or strings, as in the other instruments, are stretched from a soundbox to a distant point, *but can be pressed against a neck* to change the pitch of the note.

The lute was probably invented in Babylonia, but all the adjacent countries used it. Relief engravings as far back as 1700 BC show a lute, but harps are shown from more than a thousand years before that.

The lute and the lyre are often confused, perhaps by the similarity of the words, but they are basically different instruments operating on entirely different principles – the lute has a 'stopped' string or strings, and the lyre has 'open', or unstopped, string or strings.

These stringed instruments were the popular instruments of the times. Wind instruments were not so much used, perhaps because they were limited in range of notes and had a fairly fierce and uncontrolled sound. The simple primitive flute had developed into the shawm, which was a straight wooden tube with holes covered by the fingers, but with the addition of something new – a *reed*. A reed is a sliver of wood which vibrates when blown against, thus setting the column of air vibrating in the tube to which the reed is affixed. This is the principle of the modern clarinet, oboe, bassoon and bagpipes. Sometimes the reed is a single sliver of wood or cane, sometimes it consists of two pieces tied together.

There were double-pipe shawms and single-pipe shawms. The doubles had a few holes in each tube, not more than the fingers of one hand could cover.

The bagpipes were what they are today – a bag from which pipes projected, the purpose of the bag being to act as a reservoir of air, so that the sound is continuous and does not stop when the player pauses to draw breath. Apart from that basic principle, however, they were nothing like the modern instrument.

But next time someone tells you bagpipes are a Scottish instrument, tell him they were known and played by the ancient Sumerians three thousand years before the birth of Christ and have been played in most countries ever since. It was not until the twelfth century that they became the national instrument of Scotland.

The tomb of Tutankhamen (1350 BC) contained some beautiful solid silver trumpets, but their tone was harsh and shrill.

Percussion instruments were of all kinds, from skin-covered drums to various shaken noise makers and small bells.

3 The Greeks and the Romans

The Greeks used two main types of instruments – lyres and pipes.

Their favoured form of the lyre was the kithara, which was about two feet high and was played with one of its uprights placed against the left side of the player's chest, the strings being plucked by the right hand, and damped by the left.

Their pipes were called the aulos, and consisted of two pipes diverging at an angle, each hand fingering a separate pipe. One pipe had several holes and played the 'tune' while the other pipe had one hole only (and therefore produced two notes) and acted as a kind of drone, like those of the bagpipes. A further similarity with the bagpipes is that the cheeks were used as a kind of reservoir of air, the player wearing a bandage round the cheeks to control them.

The flute, either upright or transverse (that is, played at a right angle to the head) was known but not much favoured. The panpipes, or syrinx (a series of short open pipes bound together, like a kind of pritive mouth organ) was a shepherd's instrument and not used in high society.

The Romans liked military sounds and had various trumpets that they called tubas, one of the most interesting being the carnyx, which was about four feet long with the bell standing high above the head of the player. These

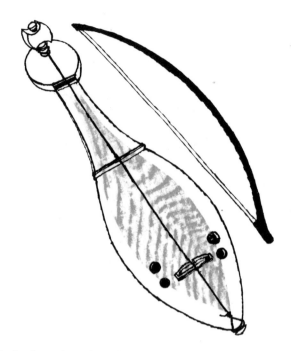

A single-string gigue from the 11th century

trumpets were limited to a few notes and were used mostly for signals and fanfares.

The syrinx, or panpipes, despite its humble usage, was to become father to the king of instruments – the organ. A Greek named Ktesibios, who lived in Alexandria in 300 BC, had the bright idea of obtaining the wind for blowing it from tanks filled with water to push the air out, and sliding bits of wood to open or close the pipes – a kind of primitive keyboard. This was called the hydraulos – or 'water pipes' – and was a favourite instrument of Nero.

4 The Middle Ages

The hydraulus persisted into the ninth century AD, but was being replaced by the pneumatic (or hand pumped bellows) version a long time before that.

Early church music depended very heavily on the organ, which was the only instrument with anything like a fixed pitch. They were of all sizes, from tiny ones carried in one hand in religious processions, to giant versions requiring several men to work the bellows.

Secular (non-religious) music depended on various kinds of lutes and harps, plus the psaltery and the dulcimer. Both of the latter are distant relatives of the harp, consisting of 'free' strings stretched across a flat soundboard.

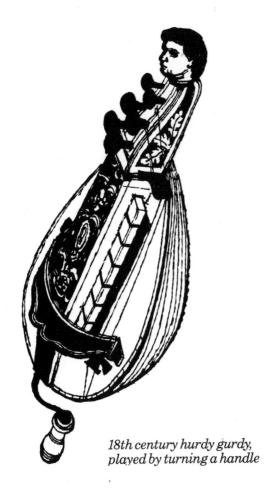

*18th century hurdy gurdy,
played by turning a handle*

The first is plucked by the fingers, the second is played by the strings being struck by two beaters.

Exactly where the idea of using a bow to play a stringed instrument came from is not clear. Almost certainly it was from the Arabs and Persians. But by the ninth century the bow had made its way to Europe and to England and it first appears in a drawing of about AD 820. But by the eleventh century it had become fairly common and a number of lute-like instruments were played with a bow. The Welsh crwth (pronounced crooth) was one of the earliest, so was the one-string gigue. The troubadours had a rather special bowed instrument, sometimes with a 'drone' string, called a rebec.

Some of these bowed instruments, such as the crwth, were like an elongated flat box. Others had a long lute-like neck and were the forerunners of the viols and violins. Whatever their shape, they were *all* called fiddles, a word which is also applied to the modern violin.

In the Middle Ages the favoured wind instruments were the recorder (or vertical flute), the transverse flute (which is said to be of Byzantium origin and did not reach England until the tenth century AD), the double-reed shawm, the bagpipes and a strange instrument called a bladder pipe, which had a large spherical bulge below the mouthpiece which acted as an air reservoir.

The 'brass' of the Middle Ages was the busine, initially reserved for players in the service of a nobleman. It was a direct descendant of the Roman tubas, but longer and slenderer. It could only play a few notes and was reserved for military fanfares. In appearance it was rather like our modern post horn.

The sackbut, or bass trumpet, first mentioned in 1494, was basically different from the busine in that it had a sliding tube which enabled many more notes to be played. The Italians called it a trombone and this name gradually superceded the other. (Incidentally, the 'sackbut' spoken of in the Bible, Dan.iii., was not a trombone but a harp.)

By the fifteenth century, keyboard instruments other than the organ began to make their appearance. The harpsichord, which was like a large psaltery with a keyboard added, is first mentioned in 1404, and the clavichord, descended from the dulcimer, appeared in 1405. The virginals and spinet were a development of the harpsichord, with the strings placed parallel to the keyboard.

From the sixteenth century onwards there was a tremendous development of instruments brought about by the demands of composers. There were full 'families' (that is, groups of various sizes and pitches) of flutes, recorders, shawms, rebecs and viols. The organ had added extra manuals and a pedal board. The lute, in many shapes and sizes, was widely used and was usually played with a quill plectrum.

The seventeenth century saw the dropping of the less flexible instruments. The shawm, the crumhorn, the pommer, the racket – all of which had their reeds inside the instrument and away from the control of the player's lips – were abandoned in favour of the flute, oboe, clarinet (the last-named developed from a single-reed

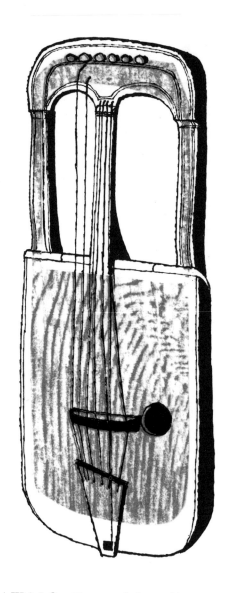

A Welsh Crwth, an early bowed instrument

shawm called the chalumeau in the late 1600s).

The viols lost ground to the lighter and more delicate-toned violin family. The differences between the two were that the viols were 'fretted' like a guitar, were played resting on or between the knees, had a flat back and sloping shoulders, and six strings instead of four. The only viol which survives today is the double bass. The masterly skills of the Cremona violin makers late in the 1600s finally finished off the smaller viols.

The eighteenth century saw the final defeat of the recorder in favour of the transverse flute for orchestral playing. The lute gave way to the easier guitar. In 1709 an Italian named Cristofori substituted the harpsichord's plucking of the strings by hitting them with felt-faced hammers and thus invented the pianoforte ('both soft and loud' – which the harpsichord was not).

The trumpet and French horn still struggled with the fact that they had a limited range of notes and various keyed versions were tried but finally abandoned for good when valves were invented in 1813.

With this invention, the instruments of the symphony orchestra were finally developed, except for considerable improvements in individual mechanism.

126

Index

Accordion 24
Albéniz, Isaac 91
Amati, Nicola 70
Aulos 20

Bach, Johann Christian 50, 56
Bach, Johann Sebastian
  50-52, 80, 91, 92
Bagpipes 41
Ballads 78
Ballet 77, 84, 88, 91, 99
Ballett 49
Bar line 40
Bartók, Béla 88, 93
Bax, Sir Arnold 94
Beatles 108, 109, 110
Beethoven, Ludvig van
  8, 48, 59-62, 84, 91, 92, 101
Bel canto 47
Bell 15, 18, 41
Bell chime 24
Bellini, Vincenzo 48
Berg, Alban 84, 113
Berlioz, Hector 48, 68, 81, 96
Bernstein, Leonard 93, 101
Bible regal 43
Bliss, Sir Arthur 94
Blues 102
Borodin, Eugenie 76
Brahms, Johannes 76, 78, 101
Britten, Benjamin 48, 94, 97
Bruckner, Anton 8, 78
Bull-roarer 11
Byrd, William 44, 45, 49, 95

Cassiodorus 39, 113
Castrati 47
'Cello 70, 84, 96, 99
Chansonniers 32, 41
Chopin, Frédéric 65-66, 81, 96
Cittern 49
Clarinet 43, 84, 88, 93, 103
Clavichord 49, 53
Clerke, Jerimiah 95
Concerto 50, 58, 68, 84, 88, 89,
  93, 96, 99, 101
Copeland, Aaron 99-100
Counterpoint 40, 49, 53
Crwth 31
Cymbals 19, 24

David, King 19
Debussy, Claude 80, 84, 103
Delius, Frederick 94, 96
Donizetti, Gaetano 48
Drum 15, 16, 17, 24, 41, 43, 103,
  106, 108
Dvořák, Anton 79, 84
Dylan, Bob 108

Elgar, Sir Edward 80, 96
Embouchure 16

Falla, Manuel de 89-91
Farwell, Arthur 100
Flexatone 89
Flute 13, 16, 18, 20, 24, 39, 41, 84
Fugues 46, 52, 92

Gershwin, George 100-101
Gilbert, W. S. & A. Sullivan
  82-83, 96
Gittern 49
Goliards 31
Gong 24
Guido of Arezzo 35
Guitar 21, 25, 49, 68, 70, 71, 105,
  106, 108

Handel, George Frederic
  48, 53-54, 80, 96, 112
Harmonics 68
Harmonica 21, 24, 78
Harmony 36, 37, 39, 40, 53
Harns, Roy 100
Harp 16, 17, 19, 39, 41
Harpsichord 8, 49, 53, 55, 59
Haydn, Joseph 58, 60, 80, 95
Hindemith, Paul 91, 103
Holst, Gustav 24, 48, 94
Honegger, Arthur 89
Hucbald 36
Hurdy-gurdy 31
Hydralus 42, 43

Instruments, orchestral 119-126
Ives, Charles 100

Jazz 91, 93, 99, 101, 102-104, 105
Jews 18, 26
Jingles 18, 41

Khachaturian, Aram 88-89
Kharaja 24
Kithara 8, 20
Ktesibos of Alexandria 42

Lassus, Orlandus 38, 44, 45
Leitmotiv 72
Lieder 80, 81
Liszt, Franz 65, 66, 68, 72, 78, 81
Lobos, Villa 91
Lurs 17
Lute 16, 17, 24, 39, 41, 49
Lyra 21
Lyre 16, 17, 18, 19, 39

Madrigals 49
Mahler, Gustav 78
Mendelssohn, Felix 8, 64, 65, 81, 96
Menotti, Gian-Charles 100
Milhaud, Darius 89, 103
Minnesinger 32, 41
Minstrel 8, 31, 41
Modes 20, 21, 23, 33
Monochord 35
Monteverdi, Claudio 46
Moog synthesiser 110
Motet 41, 50
Mouthorgan, reed 24
Mozart, Wolfgang Amadeus 8, 48, 55-58, 59, 60, 80, 93, 98

Neumes 33, 36
Notation 41

Oboe 16, 41, 53
Opera 46-48, 53, 56, 57, 71, 72, 73-75, 77, 81, 82, 84, 89, 91, 95, 97, 99, 109, 110
Oratorio 54, 64, 96
Orchestra 8, 50, 120-121
Organ 8, 40, 41, 42-43, 50, 53, 64, 78
Organum 40, 42
Overture 64, 77, 81

Paginini, Niccolò 64, 67-68, 69
Palestrina, Giovanni 38, 44-45, 95
Panpipes 21, 42
Percussion 20, 39, 41, 86
Piano 53, 59, 64, 84, 86, 91, 92, 97, 99, 102
Pipes 39, 41
Piston, Walter 100
Plainsong 28, 35, 36
Polyphony 40, 41, 43
Pop 105-109
Preludes 46, 50
Prokofiev, Serge 88
Psalter 19
Psaltery 41, 49
Puccini, Giacomo 74-75, 81
Purcell, Henry 48, 95

Raga 24
Ragtime 103
Rattle 16
Rebec 31, 41
Recorder 18, 49
Regal 43
Rossini, Gioacchino 48, 96
Round 37

Saint-Saens, Camille 48
Scale 15, 23, 24, 36, 84
Schönberg, Arnold 84, 86, 113
Schubert, Robert 80, 81
Schumann, Robert 8, 66, 78, 96
Serialism 87, 92
Shawm 16, 41
Shofar 18
Shostakovitch, Dimitri 48, 88-89
Sibelius, Jean 91
Sitar 25

Skiffle 106-108
Smetana, Frederic 79
Solmization 35
Sonata 52, 58, 62, 64, 80, 88
Sousa, John Phillip 100
Spinet 49
Stave 35, 40
Stockhausen, Karlheinz 92
Stone-chime 24
Stradivarius, Antonio 68, 69-70
Stravinsky, Igor 86-87, 88, 92
Symphony 8, 48, 55, 58, 61, 64, 71, 77, 80, 81, 84, 88, 89, 91, 92, 96, 97, 99
Syrinx 21, 42

Talas 24
Tambourine 16, 18
Tchaikovsky, Peter Ilich 76-77, 81, 82, 113
Temperament 52
Theorbo 49
Timbrel 18
Tippett, Sir Michael 94
Tonic Sol-fa 35
Troubadour 32, 41
Trumpet 16, 17, 18, 20, 39, 41, 103
Thomson, Virgil 99-100

Vaughan Williams, Ralph 48, 94, 96-97
Verdi, Guiseppe 48, 73-75, 81
Vina 25
Viola 68, 70
Violin 8, 25, 31, 53, 59, 68, 69, 70, 84, 86, 96, 97
Viols 41, 49
Virginals 49

Wagner, Richard 32, 47, 48, 66, 71-72, 76, 81, 92, 96, 113
Walton, Sir William 93, 94, 96
Webern, Anton von 84-85, 86, 113
Whistle 13, 42

Zither 24, 25